D1013112

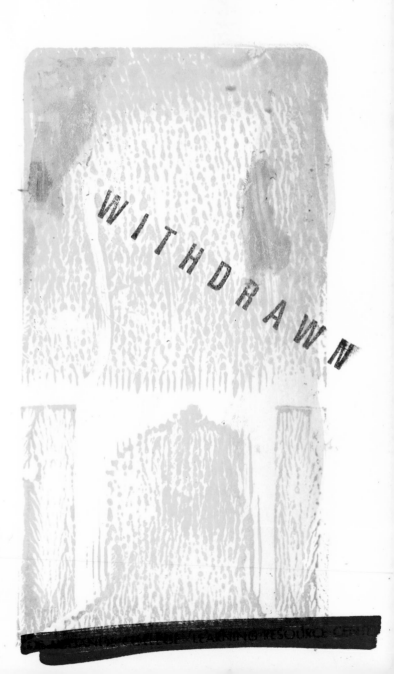

WITHDRAWN

A Short Unit on
General Semantics

A Short Unit on

General Semantics

Louis E. Glorfeld
University of Denver

GLENCOE PRESS
A Division of The Macmillan Company
Beverly Hills

First printing, 1969

Library of Congress catalog card number: 69-17339

Glencoe Press
A Division of The Macmillan Company
Collier-Macmillan Canada, Ltd., Toronto, Canada

Printed in the United States of America

Preface

"Round triangles eat pink orchids" is a grammatically correct sentence — but there is very little sense in it. Obviously, sense and nonsense are equally easy to structure. The principles of general semantics can be of great help to you in rejecting nonsense and gaining an insight into what is meant by "sensible" communication. Once you have analyzed the writing and speaking of others you are more likely to critically examine your own. You will probably be more careful in what you say or write as representative of your own ideas.

A speaker or writer often chooses words *he* feels adequately convey his meaning, but he seldom perceives that these same words might have a different meaning for *you*.

Many students come to college with the idea that life is what they think it should be and so describe it in this way. Your speaking and writing reflect your ideas of "reality," but your classmates may have ideas very different from yours. You probably already know that effective communication demands somewhat similar experiences in the minds of speakers and listeners or writers and readers. The danger of misunderstanding lies in the fact that in writing and speaking most of us unconsciously tend to substitute personal judgments for observed facts and often select only those facts that tend to support our own opinions.

The study of general semantics is not purely negative in its ends. Careful evaluation, resulting in a "delayed response" to written and spoken material, frequently allows for approval rather than disapproval.

The purpose of A SHORT UNIT ON GENERAL SEMANTICS is to arouse in you a respect for language — with all of its possibilities, as well as its limitations — and a desire to use it accurately and honestly.

Louis E. Glorfeld

Contents

Alton Barbour

MAKING UNCOMMON SENSE

A story is told of a family who acquired a new robot for doing housework. The robot had a row of buttons on its back; whenever a member of the family wished a particular task done, he simply pushed the correct button for dishwashing, lawn raking, etc. If he pushed the wrong button, however, he got the wrong response for the job.

Language, like the robot, is of little value until we learn to use it properly and to recognize its limitations. In a sense, the words at our command are like buttons on our backs. Some are appropriate and help us get our jobs done. Some are inappropriate and evoke the wrong responses.

The following essay by Alton Barbour discusses how words can be appropriate or inappropriate, and emphasizes the importance of thoughtful communication. Dr. Barbour is a member of the Department of Speech at the University of Denver.

Making Uncommon Sense

ALTON

BARBOUR

In his book, *Patterns of Discovery*, N. R. Hanson asks an interesting question. He asks first that the reader imagine two early astronomers standing on a hillside watching the dawn. One of the men is Tycho Brahe who believed that the Earth was fixed and that the other celestial bodies moved around it. The other man was Johannes Kepler who believed that the Earth circled the Sun. Hanson's question was the following one. Since the two men have different world views and different ways of interpreting the same event, would they see the same thing in the east at dawn? Hanson's answer was both yes and no. They would both be visually aware of the same object, a brilliant yellow-white disc centered between color patches of blue and green. But beyond the physical state, it would be a different experience for the two men, for their *ways* of seeing would be different.

Our backgrounds, knowledge, and beliefs influence our understandings and interpretations of events. What we "see" is affected by what we bring into the situation to "see" it with.

Printed by permission of the author, University of Denver, Denver, Colorado.

Does a skilled woodsman "see" the wilderness the same way a weekend camper does? We need only go into the wilderness with someone skilled in nature study to be impressed with how much more and how differently he "sees" than we do, even though we look at the same things. And this applies to others things as well. Does a surgeon see the human body the same way an athletic coach does? Is rain the same for farmers as it is for city dwellers? Is the passage of time the same for Arabians as it is for Chinese?

The attempt here is not to abuse the word "see" but to point out that though there are similarities in the ways we look at things and events, there are some enormous differences as well. The differences exist because the backgrounds that are brought to bear on the experiences are so dissimilar. It might be said that no one person views or understands or "lives" in quite the same world as anyone else because of the uniqueness of his life compared to the lives of others.

There is no inherent difficulty with this uniqueness. If dawn, good food, and pretty girls were the same for everyone, it would be a dismal, monotonous world. Walter Lippman has said that when we all think alike, no one thinks much. However, problems can arise from our assuming that people should see things our way, and that if they do not, they are wrong.

If this principle of uniqueness of background and subsequent uniqueness of understanding holds true, then it is quite possible that a person with one kind of background might have some difficulty in accepting the descriptions, statements, or conclusions of another person with a different background and a different way of viewing the world. In fact it might be said that the more dissimilar their backgrounds, the less likely it is that they will understand one another.

For instance, Dr. Ian Stevenson tells of a Dutchman living in the East Indies who once tried to tell a native of Java that in Holland the water sometimes got so hard that people could walk on it. The Javan immediately was convulsed with laughter and the Dutchman could not proceed with his explanation.

Imagine yourself in the position of explaining something to someone whose background is totally different. How does one explain the depression of the "thirties" to a teenager who lives in a world of affluence, or folk rock music to an old age pensioner, or civil rights to a segregationist, or death to a child? It is probably safe to say that the greater the overlap of experience, the more likely it is there will be basis for a commonality of understanding, and the less the overlap of experience, the less likely the basis for understanding. We might call this "semantic distance."

There are numerous instances on record in which this "semantic distance" has been a barrier to communication and has hindered scientific progress. For example, in the seventeenth and eighteenth centuries, leading scientists such as Pierre Gassendi and Antoine Lavoisier refused to believe that there were meteorite showers on France. Stones could not fall out of the sky, they said, because there were no stones in the sky. Theodore Gordon has described the closed-mindedness of scientists to discoveries of bacteria and anesthetics. Mausner and Mausner have documented public resistance to fluorides, even though research dating back to 1908 has indicated that fluoride does no harm and is useful in reducing dental cavities. The world has greeted with equal resistance and skepticism, hypnotism, the phonograph, atomic fission, relativity, and evolution.

Thus far we have considered how "semantic distance" has blocked progress in science and technology. To remove this idea from the realm of science and apply it to everyday living, daily through the mass media we are made increasingly aware of the obvious lack of communication between individuals, groups, and nations, and the resultant lack of understanding. This lack of understanding reveals itself in conflict about political, religious, moral, and ethical beliefs evidenced in riots, protests, and wars. The misunderstandings and disagreements demonstrate how differently the world is viewed and interpreted. The tremendous expense of civil and social disorder and the grotesque suffering and death from wars impresses us even more with the need for better communication and understanding. This is more easily talked about than brought about. However, what is said about something quite often has a great deal to do with what is done about it.

It has been said that man is the only animal who can talk himself into trouble. Much of what has been described thus far is as much a matter of talking about the world as of viewing it. Quite often our words for talking about something influence our way of seeing it, for they too are something that we bring into the situation and with which we understand it.

For the sake of exploring how our words affect our perceptions, it might be said that theoretically we all live simultaneously in two worlds, a physical world, and a verbal world. By "physical world" is meant the world that each of us sees and feels and knows about through his senses. The "verbal world" means the world of words. This second world would include the words in our heads, the words we say to one another or write or read. It is the symbolic way we represent the world we know about through our senses. In your reading of my words right now, we are living together in that verbal world. The expression "verbal world" in no way attempts to suggest an "unreal" world as opposed to a "real" world. Our verbal world is every bit as real and meaningful and important to us as the world we know about through our senses. And therein lies both our problem and, hopefully, our solution.

6

Consider first the advantages to civilization of man's ability to make words. Mankind's words allow progress. Each man is able metaphorically to stand on the shoulders of those who have gone before. Each man need not start at the beginning or continue to make the same mistakes if he heeds the verbal accounts of others. Our civilizations and cultures are as much constructed of the words we say as the bricks we lay, but in both instances, what is achieved is built upon a foundation others have laid before. Thus the advancement of science, the humanities, philosophy, the professions, and the institutions of man. The verbal world allows man to rule the Earth and seek the stars. It is what makes him human. But for all of the obvious advantages of man's ability to symbolize, there are less obvious limitations. The whole matter can be summarized by saying that words are simply inadequate to describe the world we live in.

The late Irving Lee at Northwestern University used to have his students tell him about a pencil he held in his hand. He wrote on the blackboard the things the students could tell him about the pencil. As they told him more and more, he would run out of blackboard space and would begin to write on the walls, the door, and the floor until every student finally realized that they could talk about the details and characteristics of the pencil forever if they wanted to. The pencil, just like all of our objective reality, had an infinity of characteristics. Can anything with an infinity of characteristics be reduced to words?

That is only one problem in making the words correspond to the physical world. Let's turn now to how well we can do with simple and larger more significant details and characteristics. You know what a paper clip looks like. Could you describe it? Could you give someone instructions on how to draw it?

You've seen mousetraps. Can you explain how the mechanism of a mousetrap works? Could you tell someone how to tie a clove hitch knot? All of these attempts to reduce reality to words present problems, and yet all of them are very simple articles or processes. The problems are compounded if the article or process is made more elaborate. Can you explain the Doppler effect, logarithms, mitosis, Mendel's law, DNA, the Fitzgerald contraction, or Boolean algebra? Obviously it is possible because someone has done it. But is it like describing a paper clip? Hardly!

Moving to other aspects of how words describe the world we live in, consider not what goes on outside your skin, but what goes on inside. Could you tell someone of your toothache so he would understand it? Can a woman ever really explain to a man what giving birth is like? Moving from physical feeling to emotional feeling, can you explain your fears, your anxieties, your sadnesses? Can you relate to another person the affection or love you feel so the other person understands it the same way you do? We have a hard time with paper clips, but with feelings and emotions, the job is immeasurably more difficult.

Let's take the whole idea one step farther. Consider the aspects of the verbal world that do not exist in the real world and which we do not know about experientially, but only intellectually. Some words we use describe ideas or concepts that do not exist physically. Can you explain justice, honor, virtue, or truth? Can you explain existentialism, transcendentalism, or divinity? It seems that describing the way one views the physical world with its infinity of characteristics presents a host of difficulties, but the farther one strays into feelings, emotions, or the purely intellectual, the more impossible the task becomes. And aren't those words "real" for us?

A natural reaction at this point is: "But don't we all know what words mean? And if we don't, can't we just go to the dictionary to find out? Isn't that what dictionaries are for — to tell us the 'right' meanings of words?" Ah, if it were only that simple! How do we know what words mean? How do we learn our language? We learn it from those who raise us as children and from the experiences we associate with language usage. Are our experiences with language the same? Of course not, even for identical twins. Then will we all have the same meanings for words? Again, of course not. This problem of differing meanings for the same words in our verbal world is much the same as our discussion of different ways of viewing the same event in the physical world. The more similar the word-experience association, the more similar the meaning, and the more different the word-experience association, the more different the meaning. This is the "semantic distance" mentioned previously.

Borrowing an example from Ward S. Miller, what is the meaning of the word "lake"? There are essentially two kinds of meanings, connotative and denotative. For the denotative meaning you would look in the dictionary and find that it says, "an inland body of standing water," or something similar. However, scientific philosophers such as Bridgeman, Whitehead, and Lundberg have suggested that if we want to know what a word means to a man, we should not ask him what it means, but watch how he behaves with the word.

As to the connotative, if someone says "lake" to you, you are likely to associate the word not with dictionaries, but with your experience with the word and a lake with which you are familiar. It may be a lake where you live or grew up, and one that you associate with swimming, boating, water-skiing, summer picnics, or perhaps a drowning you witnessed when you were a child. In this case, that is what lake means to you connotatively. You have your own unique and personal meaning for the word, and no one else's is quite the same as yours.

Saying words to one another is no assurance that the meaning will be the same. "Lake" will mean a different thing to a boy from Arizona than it will to a boy from Wisconsin. "Nigger" means a different thing to a Negro than it does to a white person, and the difference is not in the dictionary, but in the experiences with the word.

If we react emotionally to words such as "nigger," "Jew," "kike," "wop," or "spick," we are reacting not to the physical world but to the verbal world, and not to dictionary definitions, but to connotations, associations, and the very personal ways we have of assigning meanings to words because of our experiences with them.

An important point that must be emphasized here is that even though we think ourselves rational, we often react to the word as much, if not more, than we react to the things and events of our world. Our difficulties often come from our willingness to hate, love, follow, kill, and die for words alone. It would be difficult to estimate how many men have died for liberty, honor, courage, freedom, and patriotism, for words that have no identity with any action or object in the physical world, but numerous presidents, emperors, and dictators have led millions of people with the lure of words alone. Man is so accustomed to the symbolic process that he is willing to believe and behave as if words were far more than noises in the air or marks on a page. But how do we assign words to things or events?

Alan Walker Read, the noted lexicographer at Columbia University, has a story he is fond of telling about three baseball umpires who were discussing their trade. One said, 'Some's balls and some's strikes and I calls 'em as they is." The second said, "Some's balls and some's strikes, and I calls 'em as I sees 'em." The third said, "Some's balls and some's strikes, but they ain't nothin' till I calls 'em." The question Read asked following the story was which of the baseball umpires was "right' and for what reason. His answer was that the third was at least more right than the others because he seemed to have the idea that two semanticists, Ogden and Richards, have explicated. They said that there was no inherent relationship between the word and the thing except in the human intellect. We could choose to call the ball anything that we want to, but it is a "ball" because we agree to call it that and for no other reason.

If the thing that we are talking about "out there" might be called the "referent" as another semanticist, Stuart Chase, tells us, then we might better understand one another if we jointly can "find the referent," and thus know what it is we are talking about, or even *if there is* a referent in the physical world.

It might be useful to look upon this word-thing relationship as a triangle with the base missing. The thing is at one corner, the person is in the middle, and the word is at the other corner. The connection between word and thing is man, but there is no connection between word and thing without man.

Some of our difficulties come from assuming that there is a word-thing connection and behaving as if there is. We can reasonably assume that people can come to an agreement on umpires' decisions and strike zones. But we are on much more shaky ground in talking about "capitalism," "socialism," "democracy," "freedom," "Christianity," and "truth." We can find firmer footing if there is a referent to identify so we can know what it is "out there" that we are talking about.

11

There is no suggestion here that all of man's problems are verbal. If your appendix needs to come out, a scalpel is a good deal more helpful than a glossary. But a great number of our problems are verbal, stemming from our tendencies to assume that our meanings are the same as everyone else's and our tendencies to react to words as if they were things. All of this discussion seems to suggest that a useful and necessary implement in our dealing with others would be a way of making our language correspond to our physical world in such a way that a highly valid word-thing relationship could be achieved. This would be a way of reducing the "semantic distance" in dealing with those who have different ways of viewing the world and different experiences and meanings associated with their words. There ought to be a way to get together and talk sense and understand one another, and it doesn't seem as if we are doing a very good job of that right now. Methods of approaching the study of meaning do exist. It seems reasonable to say that the consciousness of word-thing relationships these methods focus on hold considerable potential for better communication and better understanding.

One such approach was originated by a Polish count named Alfred Korzybski who was concerned with some of the problems of man which were essentially verbal in nature. He believed that a system might be devised for improving man's way of relating his words to his objective reality. He called this system "general semantics." This book is about "general semantics," a way of understanding meaning. It is not about the denotative approach to meanings in dictionaries, but about meanings in people. It is concerned with the relationships of language to "reality" as we know it and with our behavior toward language.

General semantics may not save the world from wars, riots, and epidemics. But it can make a difference in your life. If you are willing to study and explore the principles of general semantics and make them a part of your behavior, they can influence the accuracy with which you think and talk. They can help you eliminate language habits which cause confusion and misunderstanding.

Some people are bound to say that appropriate use of language is simply "common sense." Judging our human condition from television and newspaper accounts, such language usage is not at all that "common." If sanity is at all synonymous in our verbal world with appropriateness, general semantics can make you more sane. This book is about communication and understanding, something we need more of in this world. It is about how to make sense, "uncommon sense."

Questions for Discussion

1. How can "semantic distances" bring about misunderstanding and disagreement? Explain your answer by citing current Negro-white, liberal-

conservative, young-old, or student-faculty conflicts.

2. We talk about "sunrise" and "sunset" even though we *know* that the sun does not actually rise or set. We talk about "dew fall" even though we *know* that the dew does not, in fact, fall. What other common situations are there in your experience in which the words do not fit the facts?

3. *(a)* S. I. Hayakawa says that dictionaries are not law books but history books. What does he mean by that?

    (b) Alan Walker Read is a lexicographer, a person responsible for putting words in dictionaries. How is this done, and what does it have to do with Hayakawa's statement?

4. Words have a great deal to do with what we "know," but to what extent do they affect us on the "feeling level"?

5. "It took me years to understand that words are often as important as experience, because words make experience last." (W. Morris, *North Toward Home*) What are the implications of this statement for a primitive society? For a modern society?

Writing Assignments

1. Read the widely anthologized poem "Ode" by Arthur O'Shaughnessy. What does it say about the people who are word-users (music-makers) and their potential for changing civilizations? Do you agree or disagree? Using current practical examples, build a case supporting or disproving the essential statement of the poem.

2. Prepare a report analyzing television commercials in which the viewing public is sold a word instead of a thing. Look particularly at commercials dealing with toothpaste, gasoline, and cigarettes.

3. Write what you believe to be an accurate evaluation of yourself. Then get together with another student who has also written an evaluation of himself. Discuss the bases and reasons for your judgments. Are they false-to-fact? Are they temporary? Do they conflict with evaluations others would make of you?

4. If "love" describes positive feelings about someone and "hate" describes negative feelings about someone, what is "jealousy"? Write a brief description of a situation in which you experienced a feeling of jealousy. Explain how mixed your feelings were and what difficulties you had in putting these feelings into words.

5. The philosopher Wittgenstein said, "All I know is what I have words for." Do you "know anything" you do not have words for? Goethe once said, "We see only what we know." Is this the same idea as in the previous statement? Explain.

6.

> The statement
> in this
> square
> is false.

This statement illustrates the "theory of types" and constitutes a paradox. If the statement is "false" then it is "true." Make a list of other such paradoxes in which language seems to contradict itself.

Irving J. Lee

FACTS FIRST – THEN WORDS

Have you ever played a part in a useless squabble that was the result of a question such as this: What baseball player had the best batting average in the American League in 1932? Perhaps such a conversation almost ended in blows. A simple solution would have been to say, "Hold it! We'll settle it with the facts. Let's check it out in the *World Almanac*." Sometimes such an argument can be exciting even though relatively unimportant. When more serious matters are at issue, however, squabbles can turn into riots or wars.

In his essay, "Facts First — Then Words," Irving J. Lee explains that when we look to facts before speaking or reacting, we begin to control our own destiny. When we reverse this order and talk first, however, the result is often disaster.

The late Irving J. Lee was a professor at Northwestern University and former president of the International Society for General Semantics. His publications include, *Language Habits in Human Affairs, Language of Wisdom and Folly*, and *How Do You Talk About People.*

Facts First — Then Words

IRVING J.

LEE

Two Patterns

It should be apparent that the imposition of language patterns of "completeness," "permanence," and "sameness" on a world of infinite complexity, process, and differences must result in impairing our ability to evaluate properly and adjust ourselves to that world. If a language structure does not fit the facts of experience, then we should expect to find its users talking about what is actually non-existent, and suffering from delusional states of their own making.

A direct attack on our disordered modes of response involves, then, a reordering of our usual habits of observing and talking. This reorientation would make us go to life facts first, before we spoke about them. Our existing patterns usually reverse this order, with speech first, neglecting the facts sometimes until later, and very often entirely.

In the life history of a child the facts are experienced long before he begins to verbalize about them. He wiggles his toes

Pages 117-148 from *Language Habits in Human Affairs* by Irving J. Lee, Copyright 1941 by Harper & Row, Publishers, Incorporated. Reprinted by permission of the publishers.

before he learns how to name them. But once he has command over the flow of words there is nothing in the nature of facts to force him to take them into account. Indeed, it may be more immediately satisfying to dodge the labor of going to the facts.

Aristotle was no child when he wrote about the emptiness in the back of a man's head and the single circular suture in a woman's skull. The learned Pliny could announce, "I find that a cold is checked by anyone who will kiss the nostrils of a mule." And Francis Bacon argued persuasively that, because of the similarity of the material, a wooden arrow would penetrate the side of a ship to a greater depth than one tipped with iron. Some observations made in similar circumstances today would force the modification of these assertions.

Two patterns thus become clear: (1) when speakers look to facts first, and (2) when they reverse the order and talk first. This is not to say that any individuals can be found who do one or the other exclusively, but that their behavior may be studied most revealingly from these points of view. We can then ask about them, do they go by facts before talking, or do they burst into speech first? These differences in approach may be clarified by some examples. This story by Edwin R. Embree is worth careful study.

> In a little school just outside Baton Rouge, Louisiana, the teacher had been hearing a class read a lesson on birds in one of the standard textbooks. To drive home a point from the lesson, she asked a boy, "When do the robins come?"
>
> The pupil promptly answered, "In the fall."
>
> "Now, Jimmie," urged the teacher, "read the lesson carefully again."
>
> After he had droned out the text a second time, she said cheerily, "Now, Jimmie, when do the robins come?"
>
> More hesitantly and sullenly he answered again, "The robins come in the fall."

20

"James, James," shouted the teacher, "read that lesson again. Now tell me when do the robins come?"

Almost in tears the boy finally answered, "The robins come in the spring."

And so they do — in Boston where the text was written. But in Louisiana, just in order to avoid the northern winter, they come in the fall, as the boy well knew.[1]

Then there is the Don Marquis story which shows the two habits of looking and speaking at work. Members of a certain tribe were being continually dragged below the surface of the sea, never to return. The remaining tribesmen on the shore could only watch these strange and terrible disappearances with fear and anxiety. Some concluded that devils, awful and terrifying, were at work. Others argued the presence of gods. Then one day an unsatisfied and curious man decided to look. He found not gods or devils but Giant Oysters. Following his report, the men went to work, and now the Giant Oysters are no more.

The two patterns are likewise revealed in the tale of the experiment performed by Sir Thomas Browne. Ship captains had been trained for a long time in the tradition that their diet must not include onions and garlic. It was believed that their pervasive odors would influence the mariner's compass, deflecting its balance. Skeptical Sir Thomas, bent on testing this belief, placed his instrument in a bowl of onion juice, after which he was able to announce triumphantly that the action of the needle was unaffected by the immersion.

Here is a more up-to-date situation. Frank Lloyd Wright's plans in 1938 for the Johnson Wax plant at Racine, Wisconsin, included columns designed for support which "were neither

---

[1] Edwin R. Embree, "Can College Graduates Read?" *The Saturday Review of Literature*, July 16, 1938. 4. Reprinted by permission.

pillars nor posts, but tall stem forms, tapering from a concrete disc 20 ft. in diameter at the top to a shaft 8 in. thick at the floor. By ordinary reckoning, these slenderizing pencils would take about two tons of weight each where they were called on to support twelve." In terms of mere talking the supports thus appeared inadequate, and inevitably members of the State Industrial Commission raised questions about the plans. However, "in an official test the column held up 60 tons."[2]

Henshaw Ward's example epitomizes the differences in response.

Imagine that three philosophers are sitting at an ebony table studying the motions of a Mexican Jumping-bean. The bean is on a sheet of white paper that is lighted by a strong electric lamp hung from the ceiling. Near the table is a case filled with small jars of several hundred species of beans. On a shelf is a delicate pair of scales and a set of drawing instruments. Shelves of books are at hand — learned volumes on gravitation, levitation, kinetics, vital forces, spiritual values, food values, etc. The philosophers are prepared to attack the problem with all the powers of their reason.

For five days they sit in session, pondering, comparing notes, thinking out possible solutions, arguing, developing techniques, laying out a program of methodology for the study of the bean — which continues all the while to give spasmodic hops.

At the end of their deliberations each philosopher writes an essay to set forth his theory of what makes the bean move. The first one argues for an Electrical Hypothesis: that some process of magnetization in growth has made the bean sensitive to the magnetic currents in the earth. The second philosopher has a psychological solution: that some vital principle in the nucleus responds to the ebb and flow of thought which goes

[2]*Time*, Dec. 2, 1940. Reprinted by permission.

on about the table. The third philosopher decides that the bean is demoniac, is possessed by an uneasy spirit which is trying to escape from the hard shell. . . .

If a man is interested in the way beans move, he ought to buy a bag of them, pour them into a dish, select the liveliest one, and cut it open. Inside he will find a small larva that is wriggling vigorously. In every other active bean he will find a similar larva. He can prove by a few observations that the motion is always caused by the activity of one of these little caterpillars. If he cares to study the animals, he can learn details of how the mother moth deposits her egg, what the life of the larva is, and how it develops into another moth that lays its eggs on other bean-plants.[3]

These examples not only show the two habits of evaluation, but they ought to suggest that investigating before talking sometimes uncovers data about the world which can affect our adjustment to that world.

The Doctrine of Facts First

The method of going by facts first may seem a matter of common sense, but the history of civilization contains many pages which tell how it was resisted. A long and bitter battle had to be fought by those early fact-finders, the men of science, before the power of this pattern came to be accepted. But that story has been told too often to be repeated here.[4] The problem

[3] From *Builders of Delusion*, by Henshaw Ward, Copyright 1931, pp. 11, 15. Used by special permission of the Publishers, The Bobbs-Merrill Company.

[4] See J. W. Draper, *History of the Conflict Between Religion and Science.* New York: D. Appleton & Co., 1903. See also A. D. White, *History of the Warfare of Science with Theology in Christendom.* New York: D. Appleton & Co., 1897.

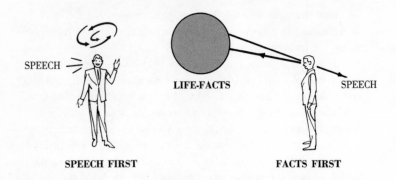

SPEECH

LIFE-FACTS

SPEECH

SPEECH FIRST   **FACTS FIRST**

may be glimpsed, however, in the life of the physician Paracelsus, who died in 1541.

All his life Paracelsus was hurling abuse at contemporary medicos and vomiting contempt at the mere mention of their practices. And organized medicine retaliated by hounding him, making his life miserable and trying to paralyze him professionally.

Those were the days when authority counted for more than experiment or the direct observation of nature. Galen had said this and Galen had said that, and Galen was always right. To Paracelsus Galen was often as wrong as he was right. Not what Galen said but what experience taught was important. To be sure, men like Bacon had been preaching the gospel of experience long before Paracelsus appeared. But it was something new for an educated ruffian to clash with the entire medical profession and to tell it that it was on the wrong track. It must have irritated the professors excessively to be told that "all the universities have less experience than my beard" and that "the down of my neck is more learned than my auditors," but it was true.[5]

[5] Waldemar Kaempffert, "Science in the News," the New York *Times*, Feb. 9, 1941, Sec. 2, p. 5. Reprinted by permission.

The medical profession was not alone in refusing to go by facts first.

> Upon the foundation of Scripture passages and quotations from "authorities" the scholastics erected their towering systems of philosophy and "science." Dialectical speculation led from deduction to deduction until the whole of knowledge was enmeshed in a closely knit web of arguments. The test of truth was not experimental verification but conformity with the opinion of accredited authority and inclusion in the approved scheme of deductions. When Galileo conducted his famous experiments with falling bodies at the leaning tower of Pisa, "the Aristotelians, who with their own eyes saw the unequal weights strike the ground at the same instant, ascribed the effect to some unknown cause and preferred the decision of their master to that of nature herself." And when Galileo asked the professors in Florence to look through his telescope and to observe for themselves the satellites of Jupiter, "they would neither see them nor the telescope."[6]

Regardless of the obstacles to acceptance of this "new" kind of human orientation, it was insistently uttered.

> Roger Bacon: Without experience nothing can be known sufficiently.[7]
> Leonardo da Vinci: All sciences are vain and full of errors which do not terminate in observation.[8]
> Descartes: It is possible to attain knowledge which is very useful in life, and instead of that speculative philosophy which is taught in the Schools, we may find a practical philosophy by means of which, knowing the force and the action of fire,

[6] W. H. Werkmeister, *A Philosophy of Science*. New York: Harper & Brothers, 1940, 11-12. Reprinted by permission.

[7] Quoted in *ibid.*, 11.

[8] *Ibid.*, 15.

water, air, the stars, heavens, and all other bodies that environ
us, as distinctly as we know the different crafts of our artisans,
we can in the same way employ them in all those uses to which
they are adapted, and thus render ourselves the masters and
possessors of nature.[9]

Extension
and Intension

Intensional orientations are based on verbal definitions,
associations, etc., largely disregarding observations as if they
would involve a "principle" of "talk first and never mind life
facts." *Extensional orientations* are based on ordering observations, investigations, etc., *first*, and the verbalization next in
importance.[10]

In these words Korzybski crisply epitomizes the attitudes
we have sought to describe. For him the methods of extension
give both clue and guidance in the search for adequate language habits.

To be oriented extensionally is to put great store in the
methods of discovery and verification. If something has been
found in our universe, then others using similar ways of
observing should be able to confirm or acknowledge it. And
if the reports have been inaccurate, checking gives the means
of correcting them. The virtue of this relationship with life
facts is that we permit ourselves further scrutiny. We need
not rest with mere statements. We can look for ourselves.
Since the process is a public one, anyone may enter freely

[9] *Discourse on Method*, Part 6. Quoted by J. H. Randall, *The Making of the
Modern Mind*. Boston: Houghton Mifflin Company, 1940, 224.

[10] Alfred Korzybski, "Outline of General Semantics," *General Semantics*,
collected and arranged by Hansell Baugh. New York: Arrow Editions, 1938, I.

and show wherein his observations fit or differ. Going by extension thus promotes the fulfillment of man's time-binding capacities.

When people become extensionalized, they are able to get out of the ruts and grooves in which their word habits have kept them. They have less tendency to take what is said for granted. The questions *who* and *how* and *what* become tools of new usefulness; and with them come the birth of inquiry, of curiosity, an attitude of moving on beyond the limits of the verbal patterns. If someone were to say to you, "This is how it has been, how the men of old said it should be done," your reply might well be, "Well, I wonder. Let's see." And in discussion of matters not immediately clear, there is little defeat and much wisdom in your adoption of the slogan of the extensional attitude, "I don't know. Let's see." We should then at least be spared the folly and stupidity that so often attend the unwillingness to go and look. For example, consider the protests and declarations against new inventions.

The first successful cast-iron plow invented in the United States in 1797 was rejected by New Jersey farmers under the theory that cast-iron poisoned the land and stimulated the growth of weeds. . . . An eloquent divine in the United States declared that the introduction of the railroad would require the building of many insane asylums, as people would be driven mad with terror at the sight of locomotives rushing across the country. . . . In Germany it was proved by experts that if trains went at the frightful speed of 15 miles an hour blood would spurt from the travelers' noses, and that the passengers would suffocate going through tunnels. . . . It was argued in 1833 that Philadelphia should continue to be lit with oil, because discharges from the gas works into the surrounding waters might drive away the shad and herring. . . . In 1881 when the New York Y.W.C.A. announced typing lessons for women, vigorous protests were made on the grounds that the female constitution would break down under the strain....[11]

The business of looking, of becoming directly acquainted with changing conditions will make evident the unending quantities of details and the necessity for becoming conscious of

THE EXTENSIONAL METHOD

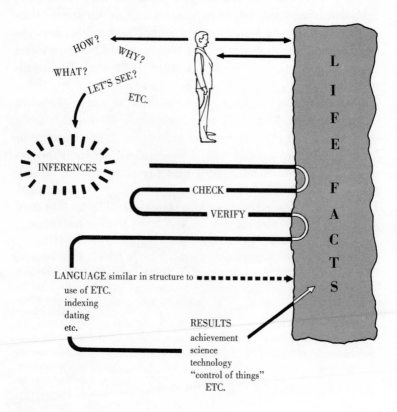

[11] "Progress Under Protest," *Reader's Digest*, Oct., 1937, 61. Reprinted by permission.

the ETC, the process character of the world which forces us to "say when," and the existence of unique individuals which are to be differentiated by indexing.

When we have become extensionalized in our reactions, we go *to* life facts (or to the descriptive data of others) prior to making statements, and we go *by* them in making evaluations. The extent to which these habits of response are learned and applied gives us a measure for distinguishing the farthest reaches of human linguistic achievement from infantile babbling and noise-making. To speak without such checking is to indulge in neuromuscular grunts and cries which may interest a voice specialist, but they help us little in dealing with a recalcitrant world.

Nevertheless, to take stock of what goes on, to attend to direct experience, to order our reactions in terms of what is found in life — this extensional orientation marks the beginning of man's control over his own destiny.[12] This offers no simple design for living. But it is a simple prescription which can be learned. There are men thus oriented in some areas of daily living in their jobs and hobbies. But, all too few are they who abide by the pattern habitually, making it a way of living.

[12] In some quarters today orientation by facts constitutes basic strategy. Anton J. Carlson (Professor Emeritus of Physiology, University of Chicago) prodded his students back to life facts with his famous caustic question: "Vot iss de effidence?" The resulting search for the data to support assertions "has launched a thousand experiments." (*Time*, Feb. 10, 1941, 44-48.) Theorists in physics, studying the meaning of their important terms, end by urging that those terms be defined by seeing what actual physical operations they represent. If disagreement arises about the meaning of "pressure of a gas," then you must move to a laboratory and see what someone does, how he measures, etc., to which operations the phrase can be applied. Or whenever you talk about pressure, you should try to visualize the apparatus involved, glass, tubing, a mercury column, and the accompanying actions, until a pointer reading is obtained — all of which is summarized in the term "pressure of a gas." R. B. Lindsay, "A Critique of Operationalism in Physics," *Philosophy of Science*, IV (October, 1937), 456.

When Orientation
Is by Intension

Today we are the heirs of the achievements of an extensional method in a limited area. The findings of medicine,
physics, chemistry, etc., have opened the way to control of the
physical environment. The creature comforts given by our
technicians and inventors had their origins in investigation of
what things were made of and how they could be used. The
triumph of our times is manifest in our mastery of certain
areas, hitherto hidden, from the depths of the atom to the dis-
tant suns. The procession of instruments, machines, and techniques which have come from the simply wizardry of dealing
extensionally with nature goes almost too fast for compre-
hension — so fast that we are likely to assume that all mankind
has caught and lives by the method. But there is too much evidence to the contrary. Men still go by intension, by what they
say, by the verbal associations they spin as if somehow their
definitions need have little to do with the surrounding world
of brute facts. Men still behave without taking heed of what
goes on, of the men and situations with which they must deal.
Even our "best" people sometimes slip, says Wilhelm Ostwald:

> Among scientific articles there are to be found not a few
> wherein the logic and mathematics are faultless but which are
> for all that worthless, because the assumptions and hypotheses
> upon which the faultless logic and mathematics rest do not
> correspond to actuality.

To talk without first observing life facts, and to act without
abiding by them — in these primitive modes of response are
too many of us held fast. The adequate documentation of this
disordering evaluation would take us away from the triumphs

of our productive genius to the heart of the crisis of our time as it is seen in the wars, in the degradation of human time-binding capacities committed to waste and destruction, in the tragically mounting numbers in our jails and asylums, in the need for more and more police control, in the persistence of superstition, bigotry, and obscurantism, in the continuing refusal to use what we already "know" for the preservation and release of human creativeness and happiness.

It is impossible in these pages to chart the gamut of intensional manifestations. We must be content with samples of some of the recurring types of situations in which people do go by words and not by facts.

1. *When people pay more attention to what is said about "things," to what they are called, than to the facts themselves.*

Note how reactions may be totally changed by a word:

> When Basil Rathbone was handed a scenario titled "The Monster," he gave it back to Paramount without reading it. A wise man in the studio retitled it "Destiny" and sent the same script back to Rathbone. He read it, liked it, and assures me on the set that it is not a horror picture. "I'm through with horror and villainy," says Basil, "a man has only so many villains in him, and I've played all mine."[13]

A friend of mine, the owner of a department store, sought to test the intensionality of customers by a practical experiment. One morning he set out at different ends of a counter piles of men's handkerchiefs. On the one he placed a sign reading "Soft-Textured, Genuine Irish Linen Handkerchiefs,

---

[13] From a column by Sheilah Graham, the Chicago *Daily News*; March 6, 1940, 20. Reprinted by permission of the North American Newspaper Alliance.

Special 3 for 50c." On the other the sign read "Nose Rags, three for a quarter." During an eight-hour period, twenty-six different persons examined and eleven bought from the "Irish Linen" stock, while but six examined and only two bought the "Nose Rags." The point of this experiment should by now have been guessed: both piles contained the same kind of handkerchiefs. The salesgirl's comment is more than a little in point, "The people just didn't look at the merchandise."

Poffenberger tested this phenomenon by giving to fifty-seven men copies of the following advertisement of a well-known razor company:

> A new triumph of American inventive genius of startling interest to every man with a beard to shave . . . for the first time in any razor micrometric control of the blade position made possible by the fulcrum shoulder, overhanging cap, and channeled guard. [A diagram showed] how the blade is bi-flexed between overhanging cap and fulcrum shoulder. It is flexed once into the inside curve of the cap. This is the minor flexure — the curve for easy gliding action and play of the wrist in shaving. It is flexed a second time — more sharply and in a shorter radius — by the grip of the overhanging cap the whole length of the fulcrum shoulder.[14]

After they had read and studied the copy, he asked a list of seven questions to learn to what extent they believed and understood what they read. This is what he reported:

> The answers to these questions showed that all the students agreed that the new razor was better than the old one, and that they would rather pay $5 for the new one than $1 or $2 for the old one. In supporting their belief they were allowed to

[14] A. T. Poffenberger, "Conditions of Belief in Advertising," *Journal of Applied Psychology*, VII (March, 1923), 2. Reprinted by permission.

consult the advertisement as much as they wished. They quoted the "fulcrum shoulder," which made possible "micrometric control of the blade position," but not one of them could explain how the micrometric control was obtained or what advantage there would be in having such a micrometric control. They believed that the "channeled guard" was an improvement. As to the importance of major and minor flexures they were entirely ignorant.[15]

In 1935 Sherif investigated the existence of æsthetic stereotypes. He first found the preferences of his subjects for certain English and American writers, including Barrie, Conrad, Cooper, Dickens, Poe, etc. Several weeks after receiving their rank-order votes on these sixteen authors, he gave sixteen prose passages, *all written by Stevenson,* but after each passage was written the name of one of the authors in the original list. The subjects were asked to rank the writings in terms of their literary merit. As far as was known, no one of the subjects realized the deception.

Some of the subjects said they had ignored the names appended. As a result, their correlation between the preference for the writers and the preference for the merit of the writing was zero. However, for the remaining nearly two hundred subjects, the average correlation was $+.46$. Passages attributed to highly rated writers were considered "good," while passages attributed to lowly rated writers were thought to be "bad."

One conclusion is inevitable. Since the passages were all from Stevenson, the rating of the passages in terms of favored and unfavored authors' *names* indicated that the responses were to the names and not to the passages.[16]

---

[15] *Ibid.*

[16] M. Sherif, "An Experimental Study of Stereotypes," *Journal of Abnormal and Social Psychology,* XXIX (Jan.-March, 1935), 371-375.

In another study along this line, Boldyreff and Sorokin found marked responses to the æsthetic opinions of musical "experts." Two phonograph records of the same recording were played for a number of students. The suggestion was then made that music critics preferred one of the records, as if they were different recordings. A large majority of the students then "heard" two different recordings and indicated that the "one" was to be preferred. They were surely responding to the names and assertions of the critics rather than to the music.[17]

Bernays tells of responses to words even in moments of crisis.

> In Great Britain, during the war, the evacuation hospitals came in for a considerable amount of criticism because of the summary way in which they handled their wounded. It was assumed by the public that a hospital gives prolonged and conscientious attention to its patients. When the name was changed to evacuation posts, the critical reaction vanished. No one expected more than an adequate emergency treatment from an institution so named. The cliché hospital was indelibly associated in the public mind with a certain picture.[18]

On one occasion at least the influence of a word has been fatal. A certain man in Germany was preparing to meet and welcome his son, who had been gone for many years. The house was being readied, food was stored, arrangements were made for a large party with many invited guests, the boy's room was

[17] J. W. Boldyreff and P. A. Sorokin, "An Experimental Study of the Influence of Suggestion on the Discrimination and the Valuation of People," *American Journal of Sociology*, XXXVII (1932), 720-737.

[18] Edward L. Bernays, *Propaganda*. New York: Horace Liveright, 1928, 51. Reprinted by permission.

fixed up, and the old man's expectations ran high. On the day fixed for his return, a telegram came saying that the boy was *ungekommt* (dead), whereupon the father himself fell over dead. That afternoon the boy arrived. The telegram should have read, he has *angekommt* (arrived).

The consequences of such automatic reaction to words cannot be underestimated if we see how the failure to observe the order of facts first produces misevaluation. Readers might ponder the effects of such orientation on the quality of our larger political and social decisions. When individuals are so oriented that their acts of judgment in connection with simple and unimportant matters are rendered impractical and useless as guides to proper evaluation, we should be little surprised (though greatly worried) if their judgments are equally distorted and unfounded in more significant matters.

2. *When the response is to words as if they were something more, as if they need not be considered as forms of representation.*

We refer here to a kind of naive, though by no means less disordered, type of reaction which somehow sees in the words themselves the very "things" which the words are intended to represent. The mechanism appears in the disturbance of the girl who "just can't stand stories about blood and death," and in the terror of the man who "breaks out in a cold sweat whenever they mention airplane crashes" because, as he says, "I see again the earth coming up to meet me just as that time." Martin Wolfson's mother provides an excellent illustration.

> A play called *Gabrielle* . . . was based on a Thomas Mann short story which takes place in one of Mr. Mann's perennial TB sanatoria on a Swiss mountain peak. In it was an actor named Martin Wolfson.

When Wolfson landed the job in the show he went home to tell his mother. She asked him what the play was about.

"Oh," Martin replied, "it takes place in a sanatorium and there are a lot of sick people in it."

"What's the matter with them?" asked ma.

"Well, they've got tuberculosis, and some of them have social diseases, syphilis and so on."

"Please, Martin," said the old lady, "please. Be careful."[19]

In this category also should be placed the experience G. K. Chesterton had with a woman selling fish. Strolling by, he stopped quickly, and pointing to her, said, "You are a noun, a verb, and a preposition." The woman was taken aback. Wherewith Chesterton began again, "You are an adjective, an adverb, and a preposition. You are a pronoun. . . ." But by that time the woman had lost patience and, as she called the police, struck Chesterton squarely with a flounder.

The crew in Lewis Carroll's "The Bellman's Speech" seemed satisfied with words only.

> He had bought a large map
> representing the sea,
> Without the least vestige of land;
> And the crew were much pleased
> when they found it to be
> A map they could all understand.

The literature dealing with the inducement of "emotion" in subjects in experimental situations shows in clear-cut fashion how reactions of all sorts can be set off by mere utterances without efforts on the part of the subjects to find out what the

[19] Robert Rice, "Broadway Report." Excerpt from *PM*, April 1, 1941, 22, copyrighted by The Newspaper PM, Inc., N.Y. Reprinted by special permission of the copyright owners.

36

words represent in a particular situation. We are saying that the very responses of the subjects which made them useful in the situation should be recognized as disordered to start with. For individuals to react simply because another individual talks, without waiting to understand the life facts he is talking about, is to demonstrate sharply the neglect of extensional procedures and to reveal how unwittingly "scientists" themselves help to establish, or at least do little to prevent, disorienting modes of response. From this point of view, read carefully this typical example.

In a dark, quiet room the investigators put the patient on his back. They passed a slender tube through one nostril into his stomach, so that a sample of the stomach fluid could be tapped at any time. They talked soothingly to him, urged him to relax and think peaceful thoughts. When he was in a good frame of mind they took a stomach sample. Then they began to talk with him about other things (with the tube through his nostril he could talk well enough) — unpleasant things, things that made him resentful, anxious, angry, frustrated. They continued their calculated tactlessness till his voice and manner showed that he was in a good dither. Then they took another stomach sample. The experience was painful but it served the cause of science.

This experiment . . . was intended to measure something that psychologists and doctors have long believed and all sufferers knew anyway — that distressing emotions cause increased amounts of hydrochloric acid to be poured out in the stomach, are thus linked to such stomach disorders as "heartburn," dyspepsia, gastric ulcer. The experimenters were Drs. Bela Mittelman of New York Post-Graduate Hospital and Harold Wolff of Cornell Medical College. Not only did they find that emotion induced increase of stomach acid, but they also measured the increase.[20]

[20] *Time*, Sept. 16, 1940, 50. Reprinted by permission.

Again, the pattern of response by which words are taken for granted is revealed in the prevalence of accounts of happenings which are passed from person to person on the unstudied assumption that they originated from observed life facts. An excellent illustration of intensional rumor-mongering ferreted out by an extensionally oriented listener appears in a newspaper column by Ben Hecht:

I heard [a legend] first from a writer named Charles Boswell who lives at 260 W. 11th St., N.Y. Mr. Boswell believed the story and related it as follows:

A Brooklyn woman put her cat in a cat and dog hospital. It died and she called for its remains. She wished to bury the pet herself. The dead cat was put in a neat box and the lady started for home. On the way she stopped in Stern's department store on 42nd St. to make some purchases. While shopping she noticed suddenly that the box she had placed on the counter near her was gone. Store detectives began a search for the missing dead cat. Ten minutes later a woman was found slumped on the floor of a telephone booth. Beside her was the box, just opened, and the feline corpse staring out of it. The woman was dead. She was immediately identified as a notorious shoplifter for whom this and other emporiums had been gunning these last six months. She had obviously stolen the box, taken it to a telephone booth to open, sighted the dead cat and fallen lifeless to the floor with a heart attack — the victim of a macabre justice.

Mr. Boswell said the story had been told him by two actors in the apartment above him, Oscar Stirling and his wife Edna Peckham, recently on view in *Kind Lady*. Mr. Boswell said these two knew the full truth of the story.

Interview with the Stirlings revealed that they had got the story from their Christian Science practitioner, a Mr. Charles Simmonds of 450 W. 24th St. Mr. Simmonds, a man not to be doubted, had told them the story as gospel.

Mr. Simmonds repeated this gospel. He had heard it, he

said, from a woman who was a friend of the dead cat's owner. This woman was Mrs. Katherine Luebbers of 28 Mile Square Rd. in Yonkers. Mrs. Luebbers would give me the names of all the people involved.

And Mrs. Luebbers turned out to be full of the dead-cat wonder. She did not know the name of the animal's owner, but the story had been told her by her son-in-law, Ronald Schæffer, who knew all about it. And Mr. Schæffer turned out to know everything about it. He had heard the story firsthand from a passenger on a commuter's train whose aunt knew the lady who owned the dead cat.

At Stern's the tale was firmly, and a little indignantly, denied, by W. F. McCue, chief store detective. And at the W. 54th St. Police Station there was no record of any feline or shoplifter corpses being reported.

By this time you may have heard the tale of wonder elsewhere. There are probably scores and hundreds of wonder-lovers broadcasting it from table to table and office to office. And if you have nothing to do, like myself, take a few days off and play ring around a rosy with this Dead-Cat-Come-to-Judgment rumor.

You will come upon no dead cat or stricken shoplifter, but you will get an instructive look into that well of rumor which is deeper and more crowded with fact apparently than that other well out of which no wars, massacres or religions are ever born.[21]

In so far as pictures (moving and still) can be considered forms of representation, we should expect to see responses to them follow the patterns of intension and extension, and we do. People forget that the picture is not what it represents and so they react to it as if it *were* the facts represented. Rosett's behavior not only describes the mechanisms, but it should make

[21] From *1001 Afternoons in New York* by Ben Hecht. Copyright 1941 by The Viking Press, Inc. Reprinted by permission of the Viking Press, Inc.

evident how deep organismal responses can be stimulated by other than life facts.

> A vivid picture on the cinema screen represented a boy and girl pulling down hay from a stack for bedding. I sneezed — from the dust of the hay shown on the screen.
>
> On another occasion a colored picture of lilacs — a favorite flower — moved by a gentle breeze, was shown on the screen. I smelled the odor of lilacs distinctly.[22]

Then there was the girl who insisted that she was "allergic" to cats, so much so that she would sneeze and suffer the pangs of "hay fever" until she could get far from the "beasts." A friend gave her the *Autobiography* of William Lyon Phelps. Upon reading the first two pages of the chapter dealing with his fondness for cats, she began to sneeze and suffer. No cats for her, only words.

3. *When men, though exposed to life facts, do not abide by them.*

It is not enough to see that men speak without going to life facts, for on occasion the facts may be apparent, though not heeded.

The cliché of the therapeutists and mental hygienists, "adjust to reality," suggests that we should probably find in their patients' case histories evidence that many varieties of obsessions, antagonisms, compulsions, melancholias, etc., are rooted in the failure or refusal to be oriented extensionally.

> There was once a man who went around saying, "You know, I think I'm dead." His friends finally persuaded him to

[22] Reprinted from Joshua Rosett, *The Mechanism of Thought, Imagery, and Hallucination*, 1939, 212, by permission of Columbia University Press.

consult a psychiatrist. When the patient told the psychiatrist that he thought he was dead, the psychiatrist told him to clench his fists, stand before a mirror, and say, "Dead men don't bleed." He told the man to repeat this motion six times a day for a month, each time saying, "Dead men don't bleed." He told the man to go home and carry out his instructions and return at the end of the month. The patient carried out the psychiatrist's instructions and at the end of the month he returned. The psychiatrist told him once again to go through the motions. The reason he had him tighten his fists was so the veins would come to the surface of the man's wrists. The man tightened his fists, and just as he said, "Dead men don't bleed," the psychiatrist jabbed a scalpel into the man's wrist. The blood gushed out and the man hollered, "By God, dead men do bleed!"[23]

Those who take refuge in private dream worlds, the man who believes he is forever conspired against by waiting enemies, those who suffer from delusions of grandeur, the chronically sick who find pleasure in the definitions of new illnesses, the temperamental who dodge responsibilities with hysterical attacks and nervous breakdowns, those overtaken with jealousy, etc. — in these the intensional orientation appears at its baldest.

However varying the details of these cases and the theories which account for their onset, and without regard for the host of measures and the special techniques of resolving the difficulties so that the individuals come to face the avoided life facts, our concern here is to suggest that deviations from extensional patterns may result in profoundly disturbed states. If so-called "normal" people have moments when their evaluations show them going by words rather than by life situations

---

[23] From a speech delivered by Irving Fink, Northwestern University, Evanston, Illinois, reprinted in the *Daily Northwestern*, Feb. 18, 1941, 5.

(and believing otherwise), we should understand that in those moments they move toward the "abnormal." Indeed, they may sometimes become ready for hospitalization.

The story is told of a college girl who sought to commit suicide because the results of a "personality test" had shown her to be a "manic-depressive type." Frightened by this report, she sought to read up on "insanity" and found, as might be expected, that she had the symptoms, along with additional information that led her to believe that in her family tree were other cases of what she defined as "mental diseases." Her worries increased as her symptoms became more marked. She then talked with a psychologist, who reported:

> It was not difficult to convince the patient that the test which started her into trouble was silly and that the doctrine of the inheritance of mental disorder, as she had learned it, was a myth; that her chances of going insane were no better than my own, or those of seven thousand of her fellow students. This treatment was effective.[24]

Of importance for us is the fact that this girl had proceeded to talk herself into an anxiety state on the basis of what she read. Whatever may have been her condition, study of it directly is not the same as applications to it of diagnoses from books. Notice, too, that she was seeing only the similarities and neglecting the differences.

4. *When men indulge in verbal "proofs," instead of going to life facts.*

A textbook in Euclidean geometry will explain that the square on the hypotenuse of a right-angled triangle is equal

[24] Knight Dunlap, "Antidotes for Superstitions Concerning Human Heredity," *The Scientific Monthly*, LI (Sept., 1940), 225. Reprinted by permission.

to the sum of the squares on the other two sides. However, assume that we have a triangular block of wood with each of the two sides measuring one inch. Then by definition (or words only) the hypotenuse must be equal to the square root of two inches. But that number must be numerically indefinite, for there may be an infinite number of places after the decimal, 1.4141. . . . Nevertheless, when one lays a measuring stick on the block, the size is something *very definite*. What can be found on observation differs from the result obtained by calculation and verbal proof.

One can argue verbally that the football team of the U.S. Marines in San Diego was superior to the Notre Dame team in 1940. Thus:

> The Marines beat Montana, which beat Gonzaga, which licked Detroit, which beat Texas Christian, which whipped Arkansas, which beat Missippi, which defeated Duquesne, which triumphed over St. Mary's, which trounced Fordham, which whaled Purdue, which cleaned up on Iowa, which beat Notre Dame.[25]

By facts, however, the Marines did not play Notre Dame, and what would have happened if they had played is something which would not be governed by any verbal deductions no matter how elaborate.

Debates on questions of moment in the halls of Congress or on public platforms often reveal such intensional procedures. To get public approval for a position while creating disapproval for others, men have found that it is not always necessary to speak extensionally with verifiable statements. Audiences are likely to applaud fervor in delivery, sharp

[25] Lloyd Lewis, "Voice from the Grandstand," the Chicago *Daily News*, Nov. 25, 1940, 21. Reprinted by permission.

turns of phrase, and pleasant diversions, and pay closer attention to devices which render an opponent's argument ridiculous and make him the butt of jokes. It is not these rhetorical effects which should be condemned but their substitution and acceptance as if they were statements descriptive of life facts.

If a public speaker can find ways of making his utterance more attractive and easier to listen to, while preserving his concern with life facts, we should hasten to welcome him. But in the heat of battle, in the effort to gain assent, that concern is too often put aside. In 1885 Gladstone began his debate with Huxley against the developing scientific investigations and the doctrines of evolution, carrying on the argument with high-powered eloquence. White has described some of his tactics in terms which reveal the intensional emphasis.

> On the face of it, his effort seemed quixotic, for he confessed at the outset that in science he was "utterly destitute of that kind of knowledge which carries authority," and his argument soon showed that his confession was entirely true.
>
> But he had some other qualities of which much might be expected: great skill in phrase making, great shrewdness in adapting the meanings of single words to conflicting necessities in discussion, wonderful power in erecting showy structures of argument upon the smallest basis of fact, and a facility almost preternatural in "explaining away" troublesome realities. So striking was his power in this last respect, that a humorous London chronicler once advised a bigamist, as his only hope, to induce Mr. Gladstone to explain away one of his wives.[26]

Argument by words only is apparent in the great good humor of Jonathan Swift's conclusive proof in *Predictions for*

[26] Andrew D. White, A *History of the Warfare of Science with Theology in Christendom*, I, 243-244. Reprinted by permission.

the Year 1708 that Dr. Partridge, the almanac-maker, would "infallibly die upon the 29th day of March, about eleven at night of a raging fever." However, on the 30th day of March Dr. Partridge published notice in the newspapers that he was very much alive. Nevertheless, in *A Vindication of Isaac Bickerstaff*, Swift again with relentless logic proved that the doctor had died just as predicted.

THE INTENSIONAL METHOD

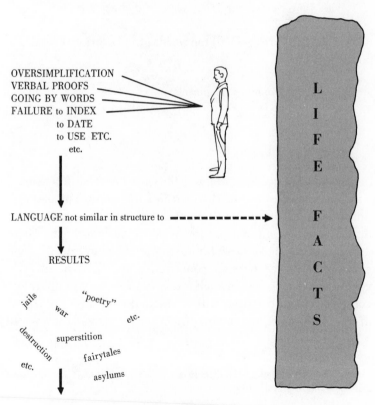

OVERSIMPLIFICATION
VERBAL PROOFS
GOING BY WORDS
FAILURE to INDEX
    to DATE
    to USE ETC.
        etc.

LANGUAGE not similar in structure to ➤

RESULTS

jails "poetry"
war   etc.
destruction superstition
                fairytales
etc.   asylums

LIFE FACTS

Sometimes documents are doctored to preserve the verbalism.

> [In 1850] Sir J. G. Wilkinson, an eminent Egyptologist, modified the results he had obtained from Egyptian monuments, in order that his chronology might not interfere with the received date of the Deluge of Noah.[27]
>
> A young biologist had just completed two years' intensive research on the problem of sex in the lower animals, and presented his report. A week later he was called in by his professor, who said: "You had better take another month and revise your conclusions. They clash with Nazi racialism."[28]

It is fitting here to recall the words of the Clerk in Chaucer's tale:

> Ye conne by arguments make a place
> A myle brood of twenty foot of space.

Intension on Purpose

Attention has been centered thus far on those intensional habits which grow out of disregard of life facts. The assumption was made throughout that such behavior was either accidental, unpremeditated, or the product of ignorance. There are, however, many areas of discourse in which people consciously verbalize without concern for the facts of directly verifiable experience. In such circumstances they deliberately contrive verbal structures without factual underpinning. These are the fairy tales, the stories of a never-never-land, of a world

[27] *Ibid.*, I, 256.

[28] J. Emlyn Williams, "Nazi Nordicism Called Propaganda," *The Christian Science Monitor*, May 13, 1941, 4.

of make-believe. Whether the purpose be the entertainment of children or the fun of spinning out a tale that hangs together, the production of fantasy and imaginative manufacturing goes apace. Winnie-the-Pooh, Br'er Rabbit, Pinocchio, Peter Pan, the Paul Bunyan tales, the Arabian Nights, Rip Van Winkle, the Pied Piper of Hamlin — these are the stock in trade of the storytellers. The comic strips, the Wild Westerns, the pulps, the patterned slick-paper magazine stories, etc., merely continue the tradition in modern dress. It is imperative that we understand here for lack of concern of the authors of this "literature" for reporting what they saw at some time and place. That they "told a story" which was interesting and pleasurable may be justification enough for their efforts. And if the stories fit no "real people and actions," we must understand that they were not intended to. For us to apply the life-facts criterion of criticism here is unnecessary. By definition, we expect fairy tales to deal with fairies and not living human beings.

Benjamino Bufano recently carved out a statue of a "bear" for the University of California. It had a beaver tail, a seallike body, a piglike snout, flattened ears, four fangs, and four flat feet. He explained the symbol to the students in these words: "Most people think of a bear only as a bear. I could make a bear that looked like a bear if I wanted to, but simplicity interests me more."[29] Which is but a manner of saying, "If I am not interested in making my statue resemble a lifelike bear, I don't have to." And we are satisfied if at the outset it is clear to all who look that the piece of sculpture was not meant to be bearlike. Likewise, it would help a great deal if speakers and writers were as frank and considerate as Bufano, for then we

[29] Excerpt from *PM*, March 2, 1941, 10, copyrighted by The Newspaper PM, Inc., N. Y. Reprinted by special permission of the copyright owners.

should not be in danger of mistaking fanciful utterings for statements of life facts. We should see the intensional creations for what they are intended to represent.

Little harm is done by mere verbalizing as long as one realizes what is happening. We should fear for the survival of the author of the following if he attempted to live by what he says:

> I'm not worrying over possible war shortages of the necessities of life. I can always find a fork in the road, a dipper in the sky, a bed in the stream, a shelf of rocks, a blanket of fog, a curtain of mist, and a carpet of leaves. — Maxellus

When Jimmy Savo sang *River, Stay 'Way from My Door* and with childlike gestures shooed the river away, vaudeville audiences laughed at his whimsy. And when in *Mum's the Word* "he performed a drunken surgical operation, pulling from his patient's insides a number of colored balloons, a string of sausages and a Punch and Judy show,"[30] his antics should not be analyzed in terms of what we know about human anatomy. His extravagance and caprice we take as such, and it is quite irrelevant to argue the legitimacy or accuracy of the performance. But it is not so easy to discover the fantastic character of much human speaking when the intent is less apparent or unconscious. The comedy of a Savo has a place and a function, and in a world beset with more somber happenings it may be that we need more of it. Nevertheless, too often do we listen to the verbalizing of men, far less entertaining, on the assumption that what they say is relevant to the here and now, when it, too, is conceived in the same never-never-land of illusion. And how often does our own serious speaking go unchecked and uncharted except in vain imagin-

[30] *Time*, Dec. 16, 1940, 72. Reprinted by permission.

ings. How easy it is to speak "coherently" by word association which sounds "good" but which is entirely unrelated to life.

Fictional characterizations, even when labeled as such, sometimes make impressions so deep that they seem "real." Only the counselors and guidance experts know how the dramatizations of "love and romance" on the screen and in novels have colored and shaped the expectations of young men and women. Because Mary Jane felt and "came to know" screen stars who tempestuously or with vast abandon made love to bright young actresses, it seemed only natural that she should wait until that happened to her. The hard-working, dimly glamorous "good" men whom she knew didn't fit the manufactured glosses, so that even though she married one of the flesh-and-blood kind, she expected him to behave otherwise. The long story of social relationships that have ended in conflict may have somewhere in the background a confusion of intensional verbalizations and extensional life facts.

It is all very well for a growing boy to enjoy the redoubtable figures of the comic strip and the robust exploits of his fictional heroes, but it is something else for him to assume that he should find the going in his own life as easy and completely satisfying. And if his expectations are shaped in terms of make-believe people, without realization of their intensional character, disappointments are in store for him.

Recent studies by Dr. Herta Herzog of the Office of Radio Research at Columbia University reveal that one-third of those who listen to radio serials believe that the characters and situations in the serials are "models of reality" and demonstrations of "what to do in a particular situation, or of how to get along with specific people." One subject when interviewed explained of her radio heroine, "She's just like me; she also doesn't want to be in her daughter's way." Dr. Herzog concluded that a great majority went to the radio stories to find ways of solving their own specific problems.[31]

The artificially engendered excitement of the night clubs, the stream of "escape" literature, the urge to get away, the efforts to speed up and multiply "thrills" may be a reflex of, and a clue to, the attempts of many to find for themselves the kind of world which the writers have fictionized about on paper. When men have drawn maps of territories conjured up inside their own skins and made them sufficiently attractive, then readers not carefully trained in the distinction between intension and extension may mistake them for the "real thing." And if the pursuit of the will-o'-the-wisp is ever accelerated so that disillusionment and frustration are inevitable, we cannot dismiss the necessity of becoming clear on the difference between fiction and life. Which is not to say that fantasy stuff should have no place in our reading or story telling. It is to say that the place of fiction must be recognized for what it is — verbalization not necessarily similar in structure to verifiable life facts.

When the Territory
Is Inside-the-skin

We come now to language uses which represent what goes on inside-the-skin of the speaker. For example, the very first vocalization of a human infant, the birth cry, the gurglings, the expressions of pain seem to be responses to internal neuromuscular conditions. Our inner states can be considered one kind of territory, of life facts, even though others cannot become directly acquainted with them. The inner experience

[31] See "Heard and Overheard," *PM*, May 20, 1941, 22.

is felt only by the one person, and we can only guess what it was like. From the incoherent babbling of the child to the sophisticated utterances of our most sensitive and thoughtful adults are to be found evidences that speech maps what goes on within.

Perhaps the simplest way of describing this function of language is to see it in terms of a stimulus-response situation. Suppose Mr. A suddenly smacks Mr. B on the back of the head. "Ouch!" says Mr. B. What does the four-letter word represent? The word "Mr. A" serves to designate a non-verbal individual. The word "smacked" designates a non-verbal action. What, now, can the term "ouch" be taken to represent? Nothing, assuredly, that can be observed by others. It is true that Mr. B. can be seen moving and his cry heard, but the inner state of affairs, which we assume prompted the exclamation, we cannot get to.

Consider another situation. In 1935 Marian spent two months in London, visiting the public buildings, churches, and stores. In the spring of 1941 she hears of the devastation caused by the hurtling bombs. The places she saw and walked in and lingered by, she learns, are reduced to rubble. She turns to people near by and says, "Oh, why do they do this!" The reports set something going inside, after which she spoke. And when Othello says,

> I do love thee! and when I love thee not,
> Chaos is come again.

he seems, in like manner, to be describing not happenings on the outside but stirrings on the inside.

From these examples a pattern emerges. Something happens, something is seen or heard or remembered, which produces effects on the nervous system of a human being. Something happens inside-his-skin. His talk then takes account of and represents it. We are familiar with the differences in a man's utterance when he is gay, sick, despondent, or in pain. From long association we can tell (though not always accurately) a cry of grief from the shout of delight. A shriek of victory conveys something different from the harsh tone of indignation. And the "Sig Heils" in the Berlin *Sportspalast* stand for inner perturbations far removed from the keenings at an Irish wake. Let us say, then, that there are vast areas of talk which can be characterized as variants of the "ouch," that is, talk which results when we are moved or affected or when we respond or evaluate in terms that do not represent any *outside* objects, situations, people, etc., with which others can be acquainted.

We have come to be able to catalogue many of the frequently recurring patterns of language which represent the

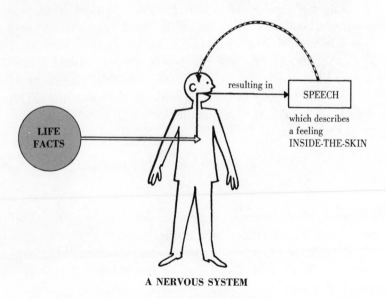

A NERVOUS SYSTEM

52

inner stirrings, such as fear, hate, hope, love, joy, sorrow, calm, apathy, wonder, amusement, indignation, righteousness, annoyance, worry, loneliness, sympathy, pity, *et al*. In terms of the kind of inner experiences the reader has had it is good exercise to try to "feel" silently and then to put into words what is represented by these lines:

> O for a lodge in some vast wilderness,
> Some boundless contiguity of shade,
> Where rumor of oppression and deceit,
> Of unsuccessful and successful war,
> Might never reach me more . . .
> —William Cowper

> I am in earnest — I will not equivocate — I will not excuse —
> I will not retreat a single inch — and I will be heard!
> —William Lloyd Garrison

> And the king was much moved, and went up to the chamber over the gate, and wept: and as he went, thus he said, O my son Absalom, my son, my son Absalom! would God I had died for thee, O Absalom, my son, my son!
> —*II Samuel* xviii:33

> Through primrose tufts, in that green bower,
> The periwinkle trailed its wreaths;
> And 'tis my faith that every flower
> Enjoys the air it breathes.

> The birds around me hopped and played,
> Their thoughts I cannot measure:
> But the least motion which they made
> It seemed a thrill of pleasure.

If this belief from heaven be sent,
If such be nature's holy plan,
Have I not reason to lament
What man has made of man?

—William Wordsworth

We should now be able to recognize the two levels involved in this analysis, (1) those affective states and disturbances that represent modes of evaluation which have an objective character and are on the silent level, and (2) the verbal expressions by which these non-verbal states are given representation.

Though we can distinguish in analysis between statements which point to objects, people, and happenings in the outside-of-the-skin-world and those which point to reactions inside-the-skin, the language habits of men in action do not make such clear distinctions. The two uses are most often to be found intertwined from sentence to sentence. A poem or argument which in one line maps verifiable situations may in the very next one be found to represent attitudes and feelings toward the situations. The task of extrication involves the sharpest and most acute consciousness of the differences between the two uses.

We have no intention here of urging that talk be limited to statements which represent what can be found outside-the-skin. Such a prohibition would be impossible even if urged. We are insisting, for proper evaluation, that statements be recognized for what they do represent. To confuse the forms is to open us to a congeries of misinterpretation. When Billy Sunday gives vent to the following:

> Our country is filled with a socialistic, I.W.W., communistic, radical, lawless, anti-American, anti-church, anti-God, anti-marriage gang, and they are laying the eggs of rebellion

and unrest in labor and capital and home; and we have some of them in the universities. I can take you through the universities and pick out a lot of black-hearted, communistic fellows who are teaching that to the boys and sending them out to undermine America. If this radical element could have their way, my friends, the laws of nature would be repealed, or they would reverse them; oil and water would mix; the turtledove would marry the turkey buzzard; the sun would rise in the west and set in the east; chickens would give milk and cows would lay eggs; the pigs would crow and roosters would squeal; cats would bark and dogs would mew; the least would be the greatest; a part would be greater than the whole; yesterday would be day after tomorrow, if that crowd were in control....[32]

we must understand before reacting just what we are reacting to—sentences which describe what can be found in life, or sentences which represent the way the Reverend Mr. Sunday responds to what he talks about, or both. To do what he wants us to on the basis of his own inner perturbations is quite different from acting on the basis of what we should find on investigation of life facts.

In Short

To be oriented *extensionally* is to realize the primary importance of life facts, to emphasize the roles of observation and investigation, to go to the facts first and to abide by them. To be oriented *intensionally* is to order behavior in terms of definitions, arguments, verbal proofs, and theorizings, essentially disregarding the existence of verifiable life facts. Fairy tales, fiction, myths, etc., may be considered intension-with-a-

---

[32] *The American Mercury*, Feb., 1925, 156. Reprinted by permission.

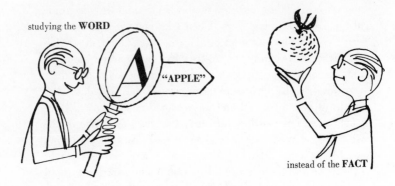

studying the **WORD**

"APPLE"

instead of the **FACT**

purpose. Verbalization which represents what goes on inside-the-skin must be analyzed as such and not in terms of its correspondence with facts-outside-the-skin.

The basic attitude: "I don't know. Let's see."

Questions for Discussion

1. Can you think of any reasons why purely extensional thinking, speaking, and writing are not always possible?

2. Cite ways in which some political speeches appeal to intensional thinking. What can we do to control intensional thinking?

3. Briefly discuss your tastes in science fiction. Might an understanding of intensional and extensional orientations tend to influence your tastes? Explain.

4. One Christmas Eve during the Civil War a regiment of Yankee soldiers and a regiment of Rebel soldiers were camped on opposite sides of the Rap-

pahannock River. Each encampment could hear every sound from the enemy camp. In the evening a Southern band began playing "Home Sweet Home." Then the Northern band took up the refrain and both bands played together in the quiet of Christmas Eve. An unspoken truce was acknowledged between the two camps and only the river kept the rivals from joining together as friends — so powerful was the influence of the word "home." What other words affect us this way? How do they influence our behavior?

5. Members of a Peace Corps program in Latin America attempted to get villagers to boil the water from the local bacteria infested ditch before they used it. The villagers refused to believe that bacteria, which they could not see, were in the water. "Anyway," they said, "if they're in the water, why don't they drown?" How would you answer their question? Do you think your answer would convince them?

6. How do we make a distinction between intensional orientation and intension-with-a-purpose?

Writing Assignments

1. Describe a recent experience in which intensional speaking got you into trouble. How might you have avoided the situation?

2. List at least one example (from your own experience or reading) of each of the four types of situa-

tions mentioned by Lee in which people go by words and not by facts.

3. Select a "Letter to the Editor" from your local newspaper and read it carefully. Have a friend read it as well. Then read it together. See if the two of you can agree on *(a)* the experience that prompted the letter, *(b)* the general beliefs of the author which conditioned the way he approached the experience, *(c)* the specific attitude the author exhibited toward the experience, *(d)* the extent to which the author exaggerated or distorted words to make his point. After your discussion, write a careful analysis of the content and language of the letter.

4. Over two thousand years ago Euclid originated the geometry of his time. He said that many of the axioms were self-evident and needed no proof. For hundreds of years no one questioned this assertion. Then, about a hundred years ago, a German mathematician named Riemann asked what would happen if we did not accept Euclid's axioms about straight lines and parallel lines. Riemann started with a new set of axioms and created a whole new geometry. Using reference material from the library, write a short paper explaining how a new scientific discovery came from a questioning of something that was previously "self-evident" and "needed no proof."

5. Select one of the quotations Lee includes on pages 53-54 and try to "feel" silently and then put into words what is represented by the lines you have chosen.

Anatol Rapoport

WHAT DO YOU MEAN?

When Humpty-Dumpty said to Alice, "When I use a word, it means just what I choose it to mean, neither more nor less" was he speaking for most of us?

In the following chapter from *Science and the Goals of Man*, Anatol Rapoport states that from a semantic point of view it is senseless to inquire into the *real* meaning of any word. By introducing us to various types of definitions, he explores ways in which to bridge the gap between words and experiences and relates the way in which these definitions fit into the "intensional/ extensional" patterns discussed earlier by Irving J. Lee.

Anatol Rapoport, a mathematician and biologist, is a fellow of the American Academy of Sciences, a member of the American Mathematical Society, and past president of the International Society for General Semantics.

What Do You Mean?

ANATOL

RAPOPORT

Let us return to our two patriots arguing about the respective merits of their countries. We are dealing with Jones and Ivanov, discussing U.S.A. and U.S.S.R., as many Joneses and many Ivanovs actually did in Teheran, Berlin, Fairbanks, Poltava, wherever they met and whenever an interpreter turned up.

As long as they are saying, "My country is a better place to live in than yours," they are making value judgments, talking about themselves. They can, of course, agree to disagree by recognizing the fact that they are not talking about their countries at all. But although it is easy to agree to disagree about caviar and remain friends, it is not so easy to disagree about a "way of life" and remain friends. "Ways of life" have a way of spreading and their spreading invites resistance. Thus, each of our friends wishes to make the other "see the light."

"My country is a democracy," says Jones, "and yours is a dictatorship."

"On the contrary," counters Ivanov.

As they are saying it, the discussion seems to be on the hopeless 'tis-'tain't level. Yet, as we have seen in the preceding chapter, there *is* an area of agreement. Both Ivanov and Jones believe that "democracy" makes a country good to live in and its ideals worth while to defend.

If it were possible for each of them to "prove" to the other that his country has some aspects of "democracy," they would have to agree that there are at least some good things in the ways of life of both. But the potentialities for agreement are not realized, because "proofs" are rejected *in toto* by each opponent.

"Ours is the *real* democracy; yours is a sham one," each of them says.

They are not communicating, because the experiences that have led to the word "democracy" for Jones are not similar to the experiences that have led to that word for Ivanov. The words are the same, but their meanings are different. The agreement on the principle "Democracy makes a country good to live in" is only a *verbal* agreement. For Jones "democracy" means the two-party system, Fourth of July speeches, stories of newsboys becoming millionaires, Town Hall meetings, informality, hot dogs, trailer camps, soapboxes, the Inquiring Reporter. For Ivanov "democracy" means the one-party system, full employment, social security, stories of peasant boys becoming engineers, aviators, and concert violinists, shop meetings, May Day parades, quick action by the state against individuals who become rich by illegitimate means (by means illegitimate for Ivanov but legitimate for Jones), and the line of people in Red Square waiting to see the embalmed body of Lenin.

Even without studying semantics, Jones and Ivanov may still take another step toward agreement. Each may ask the other to *define* democracy. But here other pitfalls await them. They may think they agree on a definition "Democracy is a form of government where the people rule." But again this agreement is only verbal. The experiences that Jones summarizes in the expression "the people rule," are different from those which Ivanov summarizes by the same words.

For thousands of years philosophers have inquired into the "real" meanings of words, with no agreement to show for their efforts. From the semantic point of view, to inquire into the *real* meaning of any word, whether democracy or tyranny, friendship or virtue, taxation or education, is senseless.

Take the word "rot." To a German it means "red," to a Russian "mouth," and to us you know what. How good a philosopher do you have to be to discover the "real" meaning of "rot"?

One may object to this example, since there is nothing remarkable in the fact that a similar sound may have different meanings in different languages.

Take, then, the word "rod," and consider what it means to a land surveyor and what it means to a gangster, both presumably speaking English. Words do have a variety of sometimes unrelated meanings, and these are not inherent in the words themselves but in their *usage*. Usage depends on the experiences associated with the *use* of words. The various meanings of a word may overlap in spots. But it is no less important to know that other areas of their meanings may be far apart.

There is a mistaken belief that the etymology (ancestry) of a word is somehow a key to its "real" meaning.

Some time ago the Ukranian delegate to the United Nations charged the government of Greece with "antidemocratic" motives in wanting to demilitarize the Bulgarian border. The Greek undersecretary of foreign affairs replied:

"Democracy is a Greek word, and Greece knows better than anyone else how to interpret it."

Sigmund Freud once pointed out in a lecture on hysteria that men as well as women were often subject to its symptoms. A distinguished Viennese professor upon hearing this walked angrily out of the hall.

"Never have I heard such nonsense," he fussed. "Men subject to hysteria! Why the very word "hysteria" is derived from the Greek word for *womb!*"

Both the Greek diplomat and the Viennese professor were making the same common mistake: they were confusing words with the things to which words are supposed to refer.

Words are invented by human beings, and their meanings are attributed to them by persons. These meanings arise out of experience. Different sets of experiences may map on the same word.

Definitions
of Definitions

How, then, can the meaning of a word be made clear? Obviously by indicating the experiences associated with it. But how do we communicate experiences? By words. Are we in a vicious circle? It looks serious, but there may be a way out.

The question "What do you mean?" asks for the meaning of some words or expressions you are using. Meaning is associated with experience. So actually the question "What do you mean?" is a request to share the experiences associated with the words you are using. In answer to such a request, a definition is usually made.

We shall examine several types of definitions and gauge their usefulness from the standpoint of sharing experience.

1. *Defining a word by giving a synonym.*

Pocket dictionaries are full of such definitions. Asked to define "man" a pocket dictionary will often tell you that a "man" is a "human being."

2. *Making a definition by classification.*

Such definitions haunt the classrooms. Pupils who can rattle off "Autocracy is a form of government in which power is concentrated in the hands of one man" and "Capitalism is an economic system based on competition and free enterprise" are most likely to get an A in civics. In the days of Aristotle (about 350 B.C.), "man" was often defined as a "rational animal," also a definition by classification. Such definitions tell first what sort of thing the word you are defining refers to (capitalism is a sort of economic system; man is a sort of animal); then it tells how to distinguish the *special* thing the word refers to (not *any* kind of economic system, but one based on competition and free enterprise; not *any* kind of animal, but a rational animal).

3. *Defining a word by enumerating words to which it refers collectively* (definition by enumeration).

Spices are cinnamon, cloves, paprika, ginger, and such.

The kings of the house of Stuart were James I, Charles I, Charles II, and James II.

4. *Defining by exhibiting an example.*

That is the way Robinson Crusoe taught English to Friday. He would point to a hairy animal and say "goat," to the strange object he carried and say "umbrella," etc. Friday learned fast. Children also learn to speak this way.

5. *The Operational Definition.*

Such definitions are commonly used in modern science. A physicist asked to define, say, the "Joule-Thompson effect" will *usually describe the experiments*, in which this effect can be *observed*. A more homely example of an operational definition can be found in the *recipe*.

An operational definition tells *what to do* in order to experience or to recognize the thing to which the word defined refers.

Now let us see how the different kinds of definition serve their purpose. We recall that a definition is used to answer the question "What do you mean?" — a request to *share experience.*

Definition by synonym is useful only if the synonym is closer to our experiences than the word defined. Sometimes this is the case. People for whom "abdomen" is just a noise, may know very well what "belly" stands for. But the opposite situation is rare.

If you have used pocket dictionaries a great deal, where words are defined by synonyms, you must have experienced the disappointment of finding a synonym that means no more to you than the word you have looked up. The disappointment may grow into a minor frustration if you look up the synonym only to find it defined by the original "sticker."

Definitions by classification are more often useful than definitions by synonym. Their usefulness depends on the familiarity of the person who asks for the definition with the *class* of things into which the word defined is placed. For instance, Jones can explain the grapefruit to Ivanov, who may never have seen one, by such a definition.

> A grapefruit is a citrous fruit, more sour than an orange and less sour than a lemon, larger than both, and canary yellow.

Ivanov has eaten both lemons and oranges. He can form at least some idea of what a grapefruit is like. The shortcomings of a definition by classification is that it does not *necessarily* bring the word defined closer to experience.

A Jabberwock can be defined by "classifying" it.

> A Jabberwock is an animal with "jaws that bite and claws
> that snatch."

But the definition does not bring us any closer to an actual
experience with a Jabberwock.

Similarly, one can define anything one pleases by stringing
words together in such a way as to make it appear that one is
clarifying meaning. Here are a few examples. It is easy to
invent them.

> An irresistible force is a causative agency, able to over-
> come all obstacles.
>
> The First Cause is that event which was preceded by no
> other.
>
> The Good is what all things aim at.
>
> The devil is a being who is responsible for the existence
> of evil.
>
> Love is that affection which, being compounded of animal
> desire, esteem, and benevolence, becomes the bond of attach-
> ment and union between individuals of the different sexes,
> and makes them enjoy in the society of each other a species
> of happiness which they experience nowhere else.

Definitions which by their sentence structure seem to be
clarifying something, but actually are not, resemble useless
patent medicines. The harm of patent medicines is often not
in themselves but in that the addicts keep hoping they will be
helped and delay seeking competent advice and effective measures. Similarly, the addicts of definitions by classification
(Aristotelian definitions) are often pedantic in "defining their
terms" without realizing the futility of such definitions.

Definitions by enumeration are useful in defining classes of things if the names of the members of the class defined are closer to experience than the class itself. A person may not know to what the Pentateuch refers, but he may be familiar with Genesis, Exodus, Leviticus, Numbers, and Deuteronomy. He may have seen frogs, newts, and salamanders, but he may not know that biologists refer to all of them collectively as amphibia.

As a rule, definitions by enumeration do carry words closer to experience, because terms referring to collections of events are less directly connected with experience than the events themselves. We have used this sort of definition above when we defined Jone's democracy by Town Hall meetings, etc., and Ivanov's democracy by May Day parades, etc.

The weak spot in this sort of definition is that some words seem to refer not to classes, as, for example, the sun, and some classes are too large to enumerate. If I wanted to define "man" by enumeration, I would have to put down some two billion names, a fourth of them Chinese, a difficult and rather useless task. Fortunately, in some cases only a few examples are needed to make the meaning of the class clear. An "etc." placed at the end of such a partial list is a reminder that the class has not been exhausted.

A great advantage in making definitions by *exhibiting an example* is that one cannot define fictions that way. Just try to define Jabberwock or the First Cause by pointing to something and see how sticking to definition by exhibiting an example protects you from believing in ghosts. However, this advantage becomes a disadvantage when one wishes to define something which is not immediately at hand or something more abstract than objects to which one can point. Jonathan Swift made great fun of definition by example. He describes in his satire,

Gulliver's Travels, how the academicians of Lagado decided to do away with spoken language altogether, arguing that

> . . . since the words are only names for things, it would be convenient for all men to carry about them such things as were necessary to express the particular business they are to discourse on . . .

Accordingly, says Swift, the learned men of Lagado

> adhere to the new scheme of expressing themselves by things, which hath only this inconvenience attending it, that if a man's business be very great, and of various kinds, he must be obliged in proportion to carry a greater bundle of things upon his back, unless he can afford one or two strong servants to attend him.

The great value of making a definition by exhibiting an example is that it does bridge the gap between words and experience. This, in fact, is the only purpose of definition. Definition by synonym and definition by classification may indirectly bridge this gap if the words used in the definition are closer to experience than the words defined. But this is not necessarily so. In the case of definition by example it is *necessarily* so, because what you exhibit is *not* a word. Still a difficulty remains, quite aside from Swift's objections, to this kind of definition. Many words refer to real things, and these may not be at hand to point to, or one may not point to them at all. Here are a few examples:

electric current	hydrogen
standard deviation	habeas corpus
the French language	mumps
acrophobia	sonata
chiaroscuro	taxes

The *operational definition* succeeds most effectively in connecting such *abstract* words with experience.

In discussing operational definitions of abstract physical concepts, Philipp Frank says:

> These sentences [operational definitions] contain the abstract words of the physical principles like "current" . . . also the words of the everyday English language. Obviously, they contain words like "wire" and other words which describe the apparatus by which the intensity of a current is actually measured.[1]

Note how the operational definition works. One cannot point to an ampere of electric current (the most one could point at would be the wire that carries it). But one does not dodge the issue by defining a word with other words without bothering to determine whether they are any closer to experience. One gives a set of *directions*, in words, to be sure, but words almost certainly closer to experience than the word defined (wire, magnet, etc.). If one follows these directions, one has the experience summarized by the words "one ampere of electric current."

Sometimes a definition that sounds like an Aristotelian one performs the job of an operational definition. If I say "Acrophobia is a mental disturbance characterized by a fear of high places" I seem to be making an Aristotelian definition. But it can easily be translated into an operational one: "Question a great many people on how they feel about high places, and you will find that a certain percentage of them will declare that they are 'afraid' of high places. Furthermore, if such a person happens to be on a roof or a mountaintop, he usually exhibits

[1] Philipp Frank, "Science Teaching and the Humanities."

a quickening of heart beat and expresses a desire to get down. Such people are said to suffer from acrophobia."

Let us see what happens when we apply an operational definition to a fiction. A vampire, for example, can be defined by a good Aristotelian definition: "A vampire is a person who habitually sucks other people's blood." If we attempted to translate this definition into an operational one, we would have to say something like this: "Have a great many persons watched at night, and you will find that some go abroad and suck blood out of sleeping people, usually from a small lesion in the neck. Such people are called vampires." This operational definition is formally as good as the one of acrophobia except for one thing: you will probably not find any people with blood-sucking habits.

So it appears from the operations prescribed by the operational definition that if any "meaning" is to be attached to the word "vampire," it cannot refer to a person (since no such persons are observed). The operations have revealed that the Aristotelian definition of a "vampire," although formally flawless, is meaningless.

Practically all operational definitions say in fact "Do so-and-so, and you will find . . ." They *predict* an experience. They may also be called definitions by prediction.

In modern semantic literature, definitions by synonym and by classification are often called "intensional definitions," while those by enumeration, example, and operation are called "extensional definitions." From the standpoint of bridging the gap between words and experiences, extensional definitions are to be preferred. As a matter of fact, if that gap is bridged at all, somewhere a definition by example or an operational definition is involved.

The definition by example need not involve language at all. The syntactic structure of an operational definition involves an imperative form of a verb (do so-and-so) and a predictive assertion (you will find ...). This structure is sometimes clumsy and may be discarded for the elegant structure of the Aristotelian definition (a so-an-so is a such-and-such which is characterized by a this-and-that); but if a definition is to serve its purpose (sharing experience), an indication of experience must be involved.

"The stockyards are an area where animals are processed into meat" is a short, elegant definition of the stockyards. But the *reality* of the stockyards is implied in another, clumsier definition, which I would give to a visitor in Chicago if I wanted to bring the stockyards within the range of his experience.

"Take the Halsted Street car to 39th St., etc. ...."

"Hell is the place where the wicked go when they die" also looks like a definition. But when you try to translate it into operational terms you will immediately get into difficulties. You will be at a loss to indicate a proper procedure in order to experience hell.

Just as assertions about things must be traced to the experiences that gave rise to them, the meanings of words must also be traced in this way.

Words which fail to show an ancestry of experience may nevertheless be well "defined" by intensional definitions, that is, by other words. But they usually cannot be defined by extensional definitions, especially by exhibiting an example and by the operational definition, because these, by their very nature, imply connection with experience.

Extensional definitions, therefore, especially the operational ones, are more generally valuable for the purpose for which definitions are intended — to bridge the gap between words and experience.

An operational definition can do everything all the others can do and often more. In some cases only an operational definition can bridge the gap between words and experience. Its drawback is that grammatically it is not very elegant. Therefore, if one is concerned with literary style, one might avoid the operational definition; but if one is concerned with communicating meaning, one should use it at the slightest indication that the meaning is otherwise not clear.

Granted that a way can be found to map experience on language, how can the infinite variety of experience to which we are subject be mapped on a language of only a few thousand words, to which the vocabulary of most people is limited?

Questions for Discussion

1. What problem arises with definitions of definitions?
2. Explain the expression "Words don't mean, people mean." How can words *not* mean? How can people mean *without* words?
3. How are the physical sciences able to capitalize on past knowledge? How do scientists define words in order to be understood by other scientists?
4. Alfred Korzybski said that "Definitions which apply to everyone, apply to no one." What did he mean? Give some examples of definitions that are so inclusive as to "apply to no one."
5. Why is it impossible to give an operational definition of some words?

6. In the last paragraph of "What Do You Mean?" Rapoport raises a significant question. How would you answer it?

Writing Assignments

1. Define the word "insect" in the five ways suggested by Rapoport.
2. Write intensional definitions of three different concepts. Then write an extensional definition of each, giving a concrete example for one, enumerating a class for another, and using an operational definition for the third.
3. Make a list of words that are limited, according to Rapoport, in the ways in which they can be defined. Give reasons for their limitations.

S. I. Hayakawa

CLASSIFICATION

Have you and your friends ever tried to invent a language of your own in order to prevent outsiders from understanding what you wanted to talk about? Whether you realized it or not, the instant you named something, you classified it.

In the following discussion, S. I. Hayakawa points out the difficulties that arise when we give events, objects, and people labels that do not fit. The higher the level of abstraction, the more complex the difficulties — and the more irrational the labeler — may become.

While classification is useful and necessary, we should remember that to say one person (or object or event) is exactly like another is to be aware only of similarities and to be guilty of ignoring differences. By assigning mental index numbers to our terms, we can avoid many classification problems.

S. I. Hayakawa is a member of the English faculty of San Francisco State College. He is also the Editor of *ETC: A Review of General Semantics*, and the author of several articles and books about language.

Classification

S. I. HAYAKAWA

Giving Things Names

The figure below shows eight objects, let us say animals, four large and four small, a different four with round heads and another four with square heads, and still another four with curly tails and another four with straight tails. These animals, let us say, are scampering about your village, but since at first they are of no importance to you, you ignore them. You do not even give them a name.

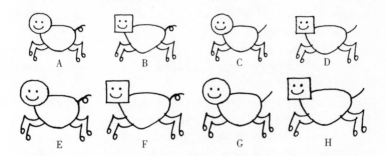

One day, however, you discover that the little ones eat up your grain, while the big ones do not. A differentiation sets itself up, and abstracting the common characteristics of A, B, C, and D, you decide to call these *gogo*; E, F, G, and H you decide to call *gigi*. You chase away the *gogo*, but leave the *gigi* alone. Your neighbor, however, has had a different experience; he finds that those with square heads bite, while those with round heads do not. Abstracting the common characteristics of B, D, F, and H, he calls them *daba*, and A, C, E, and G he calls *dobo*. Still another neighbor discovers, on the other hand, that those with curly tails kill snakes, while those with straight tails do not. He differentiates them, abstracting still another set of common characteristics: A, B, E, and F are *busa*, while C, D, G, and H are *busana*.

Now imagine that the three of you are together when E runs by. You say, "There goes the *gigi*"; your first neighbor says, "There goes the *dobo*"; your other neighbor says, "There goes the *busa*." Here immediately a great controversy arises. What is it really, a *gigi*, a *dobo*, or a *busa*? What is its *right name*? You are quarreling violently when along comes a fourth person from another village who calls it a *muglock*, an edible animal, as opposed to *uglock*, an inedible animal — which doesn't help matters a bit.

Of course, the question, "What is it *really*? What is its *right name*?" is a nonsense question. By a nonsense question is meant one that is not capable of being answered. Things can have "right names" only if there is a necessary connection between symbols and things symbolized, and we have seen that there is not. That is to say, in the light of your interest in protecting your grain, it may be necessary for you to distinguish the animal E as a *gigi*; your neighbor, who doesn't like to be bitten, finds it practical to distinguish it as a *dobo*; your other neighbor, who likes to see snakes killed, distinguishes it as a *busa*. What we call things and where we draw the line between one class of things and another depend upon the interests we have and the purposes of the classification. For example, animals are classified in one way by the meat industry, in a different way by the leather industry, in another different way by the fur industry, and in a still different way by the biologist. None of these classifications is any more final than any of the others; each of them is useful for its purpose.

This holds, of course, for everything we perceive. A table "is" a table to us, because we can understand its relationship to our conduct and interests; we eat at it, work on it, lay things on it. But to a person living in a culture where no tables are used, it may be a very big stool, a small platform, or a meaningless structure. If our culture and upbringing were different, that is to say, our world would not even look the same to us.

Many of us, for example, cannot distinguish between pickerel, pike, salmon, smelts, perch, crappies, halibut, and mackerel; we say that they are "just fish, and I don't like fish." To a seafood connoisseur, however, these distinctions are real, since they mean the difference to him between one kind of good meal, a very different kind of good meal, or a poor meal. To a zoologist, even finer distinctions become of great importance, since he has other and more general ends in view. When we hear the statement, then, "This fish is a specimen of the pompano, *Trachinotus carolinus*," we accept this as being "true," even if we don't care, not because that is its "right name," but because that is how it is *classified* in the most complete and most general system of classification which people most deeply interested in fish have evolved.

When we name something, then, we are classifying. *The individual object or event we are naming, of course, has no name and belongs to no class until we put it in one.* To illustrate again, suppose that we were to give the *extensional* meaning of the word "Korean." We would have to point to all "Koreans" living at a particular moment and say, "The word 'Korean' denotes at the present moment these persons: A_1, A_2, A_3 . . . A_n." Now, let us say, a child, whom we shall designate as Z, is born among these "Koreans." *The extensional meaning of the word "Korean," determined prior to the existence of Z, does not include Z.* Z is a new individual belonging to no classification, since all classifications were made without taking Z into account. Why, then, is Z also a "Korean?" *Because we say so.* And, saying so — fixing the classification — we have determined to a considerable extent future attitudes toward Z. For example, Z will always have certain rights in Korea; he will always be regarded in other nations as an "alien" and will be subject to laws applicable to "aliens."

In matters of "race" and "nationality," the way in which classifications work is especially apparent. For example, the present writer is by birth a "Canadian," by "race" a "Japanese," and is now an "American." Although he was legally admitted to the United States on a Canadian passport as a "non-quota immigrant," he was unable to apply for American citizenship until after 1952. According to American immigration law (since 1952 as well as before), a Canadian entering the United States as a permanent resident has no trouble getting in, unless he happens to be of Oriental extraction, in which case his "nationality" becomes irrelevant and he is classified by "race." If the quota for his "race" — for example, Japanese — is filled (and it usually is), and if he cannot get himself classified as a non-quota immigrant, he is not able to get in at all. Are all these classifications "real"? Of course they are, and *the effect that each of them has upon what he may and may not do constitutes their "reality."*

The writer has spent his entire life, except for short visits abroad, in Canada and the United States. He speaks Japanese

80

haltingly, with a child's vocabulary and an American accent; he does not read or write it. Nevertheless, because classifications seem to have a kind of hypnotic power over some people, he is occasionally credited with (or accused of) having an "Oriental mind." Since Buddha, Confucius, General Tojo, Mao Tse-tung, Pandit Nehru, Syngman Rhee, and the proprietor of the Golden Pheasant Chop Suey House all have "Oriental minds," it is difficult to know whether to feel complimented or insulted.

When is a person a "Negro"? By the definition accepted in the United States, any person with even a small amount of "Negro blood" — that is, whose parents or ancestors were classified as "Negroes" — is a "Negro." *It would be exactly as justifiable to say that any person with even a small amount of "white blood" is "white."* Why do they say one rather than the other? Because the former system of classification *suits the purposes of those making the classification.* Classification is not a matter of identifying "essences," as is widely believed. It is simply a reflection of social convenience and necessity — and different necessities are always producing different classifications.

There are few complexities about classifications at the level of dogs and cats, knives and forks, cigarettes and candy, but when it comes to classifications at high levels of abstraction — for example, those describing conduct, social institutions, philosophical and moral problems — serious difficulties occur. When one person kills another, is it an act of murder, an act of temporary insanity, an act of homicide, an accident, or an act of heroism? As soon as the process of classification is completed, our attitudes and our conduct are to a considerable degree determined. We hang the murderer, we lock up the insane man, we free the victim of circumstances, we pin a medal on the hero.

The Blocked Mind

Unfortunately, people are not always aware of the way in which they arrive at their classifications. Unaware of those characteristics of the extensional Mr. Miller not covered by classifying him as "a Jew," and attributing to Mr. Miller all the characteristics *suggested* by the affective connotations of the term with which he has been classified, they pass final judgment on Mr. Miller by saying, "Well, a Jew's a Jew. There's no getting around that!"

We need not concern ourselves here with the injustices done to "Jews," "Roman Catholics," "Republicans," "redheads," "chorus girls," "sailors," "Brass-hats," "Southerners," "Yankees," "school teachers," "government regulations," "socialistic proposals," and so on, by such hasty judgments or, as it is better to call them, fixed reactions. "Hasty judgments" suggests that such errors can be avoided by thinking more slowly; this, of course, is not the case, for some people think very slowly with no better results. What we are concerned with is the way in which we block the development of our own minds by such automatic reactions.

To continue with our example of the people who say, "A Jew's a Jew. There's no getting around that!" — they are, as we have seen, confusing the denoted, extensional Jew with the fictitious "Jew" inside their heads. Such persons, the reader will have observed, can usually be made to admit, on being reminded of certain "Jews" whom they admire — perhaps Albert Einstein, perhaps Associate Justice Arthur Goldberg, perhaps Jascha Heifetz, perhaps Mort Sahl — that "there are exceptions, of course." They have been compelled by experience, that is to say, to take cognizance of at least a few of the multitude of "Jews" who do not fit their preconceptions. At this point, however, they continue triumphantly, "But exceptions only prove the rule!" [1] — which is another way of saying, "Facts don't count."

The writer, who lives in Marin County, California, once attended hearings at the county court house concerning a proposed ordinance to forbid racial discrimination in the rental and sale of housing. (Such discrimination in Marin is chiefly directed against Negroes.) He was impressed by the fact that a large majority of those who rose to speak were in favor of the ordinance; but he was also impressed by the number who, though maintaining that they counted Negroes among their best and most admired friends, still spoke heatedly against a law that would, by forbidding racial discrimination in the sale and rental of housing, enable Negroes to live anywhere in the county. Presumably, all the Negroes whom they loved and admired were "exceptions," and the stereotyped "Negro" remained in their heads in spite of their experience.

People like this may be said to be impervious to new information. They continue to vote for their party *label*, no matter what mistakes their party makes. They continue to object to "socialists," no matter what the socialists propose. They continue to regard "mothers" as sacred, no matter which mother. A woman who had been given up both by physicians and psychiatrists as hopelessly insane was being considered by a committee whose task it was to decide whether or not she should be committed to an asylum. One member of the committee doggedly refused to vote for commitment. "Gentlemen," he said in tones of deepest reverence, "you must remember that this woman is, after all, a mother."[2] Similarly such people con-

---

[1] This extraordinarily fatuous saying originally meant, "The exception *tests* the rule" — *Enceptio probat regulam.* This older meaning of the word "prove" survives in such an expression as "automobile proving ground."

[2] One wonders how this committee member would have felt about Elizabeth Duncan, executed for murder in San Quentin in 1962, whose possessive love of her son led her to hire assassins to kill her pregnant daughter-in-law.

tinue to hate "Protestants," no matter which Protestant. Unaware of characteristics left out in the process of classification, they overlook, when the term "Republican" is applied to the party of Abraham Lincoln, the party of Warren Harding, the party of Herbert Hoover, and the party of Dwight Eisenhower, the rather important differences between them.

Cow₁ Is Not Cow₂

How do we prevent ourselves from getting into such intellectual blind alleys, or, finding we are in one, how do we get out again? One way is to remember that practically all statements in ordinary conversation, debate, and public controversy taking the form, "Republicans are Republicans," "Business is business," "Boys will be boys," "Women drivers are women drivers," and so on, are *not true*. Let us put one of these back into a context in life.

> "I don't think we should go through with this deal, Bill.
> Is it altogether fair to the railroad company?"
> "Aw, forget it! *Business is business,* after all."

Such an assertion, although it looks like a "simple statement of fact," is not simple and is not a statement of fact. The first "business" *denotes* transaction under discussion; the second "business" invokes the *connotations* of the word. The sentence is a *directive*, saying, "Let us treat this transaction with complete disregard for considerations other than profit, as the word 'business' suggests." Similarly, when a father tries to excuse the mischief done by his sons, he says, "Boys will be boys"; in other words, "Let us regard the actions of my sons with that indulgent amusement customarily extended toward those whom we call "boys,'" though the angry neighbor will say, of course,

"Boys, my eye! They're little hoodlums; that's what they are!"
These too are not informative statements but directives, direct-
ing us to classify the object or event under discussion in given
ways, in order that we may feel or act in the ways suggested
by the terms of the classification.

There is a simple technique for preventing such directives
from having their harmful effect on our thinking. It is the
suggestion made by Korzybski that we add "index numbers"
to our terms, thus; $Englishman_1$, $Englishman_2$, $Englishman_3$,
... ; cow_1, cow_2, cow_3, ... $Frenchman_1$, $Frenchman_2$, French-
man_3, . . . ; $communist_1$, $communist_2$, $communist_3$, . . . The
terms of the classification tell us what the individuals in that
class have in common; *the index numbers remind us of the
characteristics left out.* A rule can then be formulated as a
general guide in all our thinking and reading: *Cow_1 is not
cow_2, Jew_1 is not Jew_2, $politician_1$ is not $politician_2$, and so on.*
This rule, if remembered, prevents us from confusing levels of
abstraction and forces us to consider the facts on those occa-
sions when we might otherwise find ourselves leaping to conclusions which we might later have cause to regret.

"Truth"

Most intellectual problems are, ultimately, problems of
classification and nomenclature. Some years ago there was
a dispute between the American Medical Association and the
Antitrust Division of the Department of Justice as to whether
the practice of medicine was a "profession" or "trade." The
American Medical Association *wanted* immunity from laws
prohibiting "restraint of trade"; therefore, it insisted that
medicine *is* a "profession." The Antitrust Division *wanted* to
stop certain economic practices connected with medicine, and

therefore it insisted that medicine *is* a "trade." Partisans of either side accused the other of perverting the meanings of words and of not being able to understand plain English.

· Can farmers operate oil wells and still be "farmers"? In 1947 the attorney general of the state of Kansas sued to dissolve a large agricultural cooperative, Consumers Cooperative Association, charging that the corporation, in owning oil wells, refineries, and pipe-lines, was exceeding the statutory privileges of purchasing cooperatives under the Cooperative Marketing Act, which permits such organizations to "engage in any activity in connection with manufacturing, selling, or supplying to its members machinery, equipment or supplies." The attorney general held that the cooperative, under the Act, could not handle, let alone process and manufacture, general farm supplies, but only those supplies used in the marketing operation. The Kansas Supreme Court decided unanimously in favor of the defendant (CCA). In so deciding, the court held that gasoline and oil *are* "farm supplies," and producing crude oil *is* "part of the business of farming." The decision which thus enlarged the definition of "farming" read,

> This court will take judicial notice of the fact that in the present state of the art of farming, gasoline . . . is one of the costliest items in the production of agricultural commodities. . . . Anyway, gasoline and tractors are here, and this court is not going to say that motor fuel is not a supply necessary to carrying on of farm operations. . . . Indeed it is about as well put as can be on Page 18 of the state's Exhibit C where the defendant (CCA) says: *"Producing crude oil, operating pipe-lines and refineries, are also part of the business of farming. It is merely producing synthetic hay for iron horses. It is 'off-the-farm farming' which the farmer, in concert with his neighbors, is carrying on. . . .* Production of power farming equip-

ment, then, is logically an extension of the farmers' own farming operations." (Italics supplied.)

Is a harmonica player a "musician"? Until 1948, the American Federation of Musicians had ruled that the harmonica was a "toy." Professional harmonica players usually belonged, therefore, to the American Guild of Variety Artists. Even as distinguished a musician as Larry Adler, who has often played the harmonica as a solo instrument with symphony orchestras, was by the union's definition "not a musician." In 1948, however, the AFM, finding that harmonica players were getting popular and competing with members of the union, decided that they were "musicians" after all — a decision that did not sit well with the president of AGVA, who promptly declared jurisdictional war on the AFM[3].

Thurman Arnold tells of another instance of a problem in classification:

> A plaster company was scraping gypsum from the surface of the ground. If it was a mine, it paid one tax; if a manufacturing company, it paid another. Expert witnesses were called who almost came to blows, such was their disgust at the stupidity of those who could not see that the process was essentially mining, or manufacturing. A great record was built up to be reviewed by the State Supreme Court on this important question of "fact."[4]

Is aspirin a "drug" or not? In some states, it is legally classified as a "drug," and therefore it can be sold only by

[3] "The S.F. Police Dept. Bagpipe Band . . . will soon be decked out in the traditional finery of bagpipers. Pan-Am is flying over from Scotland 21 uniforms. . . . The pipers, by the way, don't have to belong to the Musicians Union since the bagpipe is classified as 'an instrument of war.' Has there ever been any doubt?" Herb Caen in the San Francisco *Chronicle*.

[4] *The Folklore of Capitalism* (1938), p. 182.

licensed pharmacists. If people want to be able to buy aspirin in groceries, lunchrooms, and pool halls (as they can in other states), they must have it reclassified as "not a drug."

· Is medicine a "profession" or a "trade"? Is the production of crude oil "a part of farming"? Is a harmonica player a "musician"? Is aspirin a "drug"? Such questions are commonly settled by appeals to dictionaries to discover the "real meanings" of the words involved. It is also common practice to consult past legal decisions and all kinds of learned treatises bearing on the subject. The decision finally rests, however, not upon appeals to past authority, but upon *what people want.* If they want the AMA to be immune from antitrust action, they will go to the Supreme Court if necessary to get medicine "defined" as a "profession." If they want the AMA prosecuted, they will get a decision that it is a "trade." (They got, in this case, a decision from the Court that it did not matter whether the practice of medicine was a "trade" or not; what mattered was that the AMA had, as charged, *restrained* the trade of Group Health Association, Inc., a cooperative which procured medical services for its members. The antitrust action was upheld.)

If people want agricultural cooperatives to operate oil wells, they will get the courts to define the activity in such a way as to make it possible. If the public doesn't care, the decision whether a harmonica player is or is not a "musician" will be made by the stronger trade union. The question whether aspirin is or is not a "drug" will be decided neither by finding the dictionary definition of "drug" nor by staring long and hard at an aspirin tablet. It will be decided on the basis of where and under what conditions people want to buy their aspirin.

In any case, society as a whole ultimately gets, on all issues of wide public importance, the classifications it wants, even if it has to wait until all the members of the Supreme Court are dead and an entirely new court is appointed. When the desired decision is handed down, people say, "Truth has triumphed." *In short, society regards as "true" those systems of classification that produce the desired results.*

The scientific test of "truth," like the social test, is strictly practical, except for the fact that the "desired results" are more severly limited. The results desired by society may be irrational, superstitious, selfish, or humane, but the results desired by scientists are only that our systems of classification produce predictable results. Classifications, as amply indicated already, determine our attitudes and behavior toward the object or event classified. When lightning was classified as "evidence of divine wrath," no courses of action other than prayer were suggested to prevent one's being struck by lightning. As soon, however, as it was classified as "electricity," Benjamin Franklin achieved a measure of control over it by his invention of the lightning rod. Certain physical disorders were formerly classified as "demonic possession," and this suggested that we "drive the demons out" by whatever spells or incantations we could think of. The results were uncertain. But when those disorders were classified as "bacillus infections," courses of action were suggested that led to more predictable results.

Science seeks only the *most general useful systems* of classification; these it regards for the time being, until more useful classifications are invented, as "true."

Questions for Discussion

1. Discuss this essay in light of the way in which you classify. Do you find any reasons for adjusting

your thinking to Hayakawa's point of view? What are they?

2. Why are we more likely to look for similarities rather than differences in people, objects, and events?

3. Can you list any tendencies on your part to conform? Why is this conformity important to you? What part does conformity play in the establishment of stereotypes?

4. It has been said that "prejudice is being down on something you're not up on." How would being "up on" something influence one's prejudices?

5. What is the function of the index numbers Korzybski suggests we assign to our terms? How practical is this suggestion?

6. To test the theory of how any word might enter the language, invent one of your own. Use it constantly during the next few days, and see how quickly your friends pick it up. Do they use it in the same way that you used it? Be prepared to discuss "your" word and its usage in class.

Writing Assignments

1. "Generalization" has been called "a plateau where a lazy mind rests." In a short essay analyze at least two generalizations and evaluate their accuracy.

2. Select one term, such as "American," "cat," or "Yippie," and explain what the individuals in the class you have chosen have in common. Assign at

least three index numbers to the term. What class characteristics were left out in each instance?

3. Hayakawa tells us that "Society regards as 'true' those systems of classification that produce the desired results." Describe both the dangers and the advantages of this attitude.

4. Describe a situation in which classification seemed to have "a kind of hypnotic effect" on someone you know.

F. A. Philbrick

LANGUAGE AND THE LAW

> If language is not correct, then what is said is not
> what is meant; if what is said is not meant, then what
> ought to be done remains undone; if this remains
> undone, morals and art will deteriorate; if morals
> and art deteriorate, justice will go astray; if justice
> goes astray, the people will stand about in helpless
> confusion.
>
> — Confucius

In the following selection, F. A. Philbrick explores
some of the practical problems of meaning by relating
them specifically to the law. In describing the theory of
definition, denotation and connotation, and the importance of tone and emphasis, Philbrick expands upon
earlier discussions (such as Rapoport's explanation of
operational definitions and Barbour's statement that
the word is not the thing) and introduces additional
semantic principles.

You may remember reading the following statement in the preface of this text: "A speaker or writer
often chooses words that *he* feels adequately convey
his meaning, but he seldom perceives that these same
words might have a different meaning for *you*." One
of the two semantic principles that have been firmly
established in English and American courts is that

meaning is in the mind of the hearer or reader, *not* in the thought of the speaker or writer. The second principle is that meaning depends on context.

The late F. A. Philbrick was a graduate of Balliol College, Oxford. He taught English at American and British preparatory schools and at the University of Chicago.

Language and the Law

F. A. PHILBRICK

Words, whether written or spoken, are symbols. They stand for or represent something in such a way that when we notice the word, whether by seeing it or hearing it, the thought of that something comes into our minds. Words, that is, are symbols for thoughts. There are many other possible symbols for thoughts. A bunch of flowers sent to a friend on her birthday is such a symbol; so is the bow that we make to her when we meet her; and so are the gestures that many people make when they speak. This is not mere linguistic theory. It has long been recognized in the courts, and a libel action can be as well grounded on symbolical behavior as on words. The courts have held that it is libellous to burn a man in effigy, and a gallows placed over a man's door is likewise a libel on him. An English litigant once brought an action because a wax figure of him had been placed on the threshold of the Chamber of Horrors in Madame Tussaud's well-known exhibition in Baker Street, London, and it was held that an action lay. Even a dash representing a name, or a row of asterisks, can be libellous, and if the identity of the plaintiff can be plausibly guessed by a reader, it is no defence to say that his name was not mentioned in the libel.

From *Language and The Law* by F. A. Philbrick. Reprinted by permission of Mrs. Sybil Philbrick. Published by The Macmillan Company, 1951.

Like other symbols, words do not maintain a strict one-to-one relation with the things symbolized. They seem to grow roots in the mind, and there they get tangled with other growing things, so that all the words standing for thoughts that are important to the thinker have associations for him. These associations are called the *connotation* of the word, and are different for every person, though the various connotations that the same word has for different people are likely to have much in common. The so-called "actual" or "dictionary" meaning of a word is sometimes described as its *denotation*, though many writers avoid this term because it suggests that a word has a fixed and ascertainable meaning common to all persons who use or encounter it — an idea which as applied to many words (i.e., the abstract words) is dangerously false.

Words not only have associations that a user could enumerate if he had the necessary memory and application, but also form secret or hidden connections in the unconscious levels of the mind. A man may find, for instance, that the apparent inexplicable dislike which he feels for a person or a place originates in a name with unpleasant associations for him. Most such connections, however, are less obvious, and can be restored to consciousness only with the help of psychoanalysis. For this reason, it is seldom possible for a lawyer to know what word-associations are likely to be favorable or unfavorable for members of a jury, though he should certainly try to exclude any prospective juryman whose name is that of any of the parties, or even the counsel, on the other side.

The study of the connection between a word and what it stands for is called the theory of definition. It is the beginning of any study of the working of language, and is of practical importance in some branches of the law; for instance, the law of libel and slander. Fortunately an elementary study offers no difficulty.

First we had better dispose of some superstitions. A primitive notion survives in many parts of the world — it is perhaps hardly rational enough to be called a belief — that the connection between a word and the thing it stands for is closer than the merely mental connection between symbol and object. Most primitive peoples imagine that the word not only stands for but in some sense *is* the thing. Such a notion leads them to incantations and other manifestations of word-magic, and is responsible for the ancient horror of blasphemy. The true names of the old gods, including Yahweh, the god of the Hebrews, were often secret, and since to mention one of these names aloud was to bring down the god himself (the name being identified with the deity), the utterance was regarded as an act endangering the public safety. The blasphemy laws enforced in recent times protected the names of religious veneration only from public disrespect, and could no doubt be justified as tending to prevent breaches of the peace, but in this they were typical of primitive customs that survive in modern time in disguise. Such Christian anniversaries as Easter, Christmas, and All Souls' Eve are the modern representatives of primitive festivals celebrated at corresponding seasons, and the pre-Christian archetypes of the Holy Communion are well known to students of the history of religion. When a witness in our courts lifts his right hand as he takes the oath, he no longer expects his god to strike him dead if he tells lies, but there are many plausible reasons for continuing the custom after the belief that it was based on has passed away.

The rational connections between words and thoughts are not difficult to follow. Words may stand for thoughts of three kinds. First come thoughts of picturable things that can be seen and touched. Words referring to these things are defined by pointing. If there is any doubt as to the meaning of the word coal, some specimens of coal are procured and doubt is at an end. Second thoughts of action. Words referring to these actions are defined by pantomime: the verb *to kick*, for example, is defined by performing the action. These pantomime definitions are called *operational definitions* by physical scientists. All physical units, such as the *yard* or the *centigrade degree* or the *ampere*, are defined in this way, and many of the definitions are embodied in statute law.

Words that can be defined by pointing or by pantomime may be called *concrete* words. Words of the third type, called *abstract* words, stand for thoughts of relations, whether these relations are between picturable things or between actions or between thoughts. An abstract word has to be defined by a metaphor — by an *as though* or *as if* process — and for this reason abstract words have no fixed or "correct" or "accepted" meaning, nor can their definitions be incorporated into statutes. Controversies about the "correct" definitions of words are usually about abstract words. *Democracy* and *beauty* are examples, and of special interest to lawyers are *freedom, justice, law,* and *rights.* The meanings of some of these will be discussed in what follows.

Many years before writers on language had clearly formulated their opinions about meaning . . . , necessity had driven advocates and judges to similar conclusions — especially those lawyers concerned with actions for libel and slander. In such actions two important semantic principles have been thoroughly established in American and English courts: the first, that meaning is in the mind of the hearer or reader; the second, that meaning depends on context.

In actions for libel or slander, it has long been laid down that the meaning of the words is not the thought in the mind of the utterer. "The question is not what the writer of an alleged libel means, but what is the meaning of the words he has used." (Lord Bramwell in *Henty's Case*). And Gatley, in his *Libel and Slander*, from which this quotation is taken, continues, "the meaning of the writer is quite immaterial. The question is, not what the writer meant, but what he conveyed to those who heard or read." A slander spoken in a foreign language is not actionable if no one present understands the language. And again, it is no defence to say that words were spoken in jest unless they were also understood in jest. "The whole question is," says Gatley, "whether the jocularity was in the mind of the defendant alone, or was shared by the bystanders." Ironic praise is actionable, if the irony is understood by the hearers, and there was a successful action against a defendant who said the plaintiff had done something "God only knows whether honestly or otherwise."

It seems to have been I. A. Richards who first explicitly declared that the meaning of a word is the missing part of its context. Because this is so, we are able to understand without referring to a dictionary words that we meet for the first time, thus adding to our vocabularies by the process that children use. When a boy reads in an advertisement that something is the *acme* of perfection, it is easy for him to guess that *acme* means summit, since that meaning is the only one that makes sense of the context. The meaning that a hearer attributes to a familiar abstract word heard in a speech is therefore made up of two elements: the meaning that he already has for it in his mind, made up of the missing parts of the previous contexts in which he has heard or read it; and the meaning that he thinks is required by the word in its present context. Here *context* includes not only the other words in the speech, but everything else that has any bearing on the speaker's intention: his gestures, tone, and actions, and the circumstances in which he finds himself. To give a simple example of what may be highly complicated, the word *hell* has different meanings when pronounced in a sermon in church and when used as an expletive on the golf links.

All this has been known for many years to lawyers engaged in libel suits. This is what Gatley says (*op. cit.*):

"If the words in their natural and ordinary sense are innocent or meaningless, still a further question may arise. Were there any facts known to those to whom the words were published which would lead them to understand them in a secondary and defamatory sense? Words in themselves apparently innocent may be shown to have a defamatory meaning when they are read with reference to the circumstances in which they were uttered or written, and with reference to the context in which they appear.

"The manner of publication, and the things relative to which the words were published and which the person knew or ought to have known would influence those to whom it was published in putting a meaning on the words, are all material in determining whether the writing is calculated to convey a libellous imputation. There are no words so plain that they may not be published with reference to such circumstances and to such persons knowing those circumstances as to convey a meaning very different from that which would be understood from the same words used under different circumstances."

"The words must be construed as a whole. It is necessary to take into consideration, not only the actual words used, but the context of the words. It would be unfair to the defendant to pick out this or that sentence which may be considered defamatory, for there may be other passages which take away their sting. If in one part of the publication something disreputable to the plaintiff is stated, but that is removed by the conclusion, the bane and the antidote must be taken together. The defendant is entitled to have read as part of the plaintiff's case the whole of the publication from which the alleged libel is extracted, and also any other document referred to which qualifies or explains its meaning."

"Where nothing is alleged to give them an extended meaning, the words must be construed in their natural and ordinary meaning, i.e., in the meaning in which reasonable men of ordinary intelligence would be likely to understand them." It should be noted that Gatley does not say that the meaning of a word is its dictionary meaning; on the contrary, he says that meaning resides in the mind of the hearer. This is illustrated in the following case quoted from his book:

"The defendant, a tax collector, having applied to the plaintiff for payment of certain taxes, was told by him that J. S. would pay them. He subsequently wrote and mailed to the plaintiff a postcard containing these words: 'I saw J. S. this morning: he said, "Make the S. B. pay it." ' The plaintiff brought an action for libel, alleging in his innuendo that the letters S. B. meant 'Son of a bitch.' It was held by the Court of Appeal in Ontario, affirming Britton, J., that the postcard was harmless in its primary meaning, and that the letters S. B. not having acquired in the vernacular any meaning as a customary abbreviation of any particular phrase or expression, and the plaintiff having given no evidence that they conveyed the defamatory meaning alleged in the innuendo, the defendant was entitled to judgment."

Two examples may be given of words that have been defined by statute. In England the Anglo-Portuguese Commercial Treaty Act of 1914 states that

> The description "Port" or "Madeira" applied to any wine or other liquor other than wine the produce of Portugal and the island of Madeira respectively shall be deemed to be a false trade description within the meaning of the Merchandise Marks Act, 1887, and that Act shall have effect accordingly.

In 1923 a company which had been selling a liquor labelled "Tarragona port" claimed that "Tarragona" was a well-known article of commerce before the Treaties, and that "Tarragona port" was not a false description provided the liquor contained a reasonable proportion of Tarragona. The English courts found against them. A more significant example is afforded by the word *Negro*. In some Southern states, statutory definitions lay down that a Negro is anyone with one quarter (in some states one eighth) African blood. A. G. Hays, in his book *City Lawyer*, tells of a couple from the Bahamas who after building a house in Scarsdale, New York, found that the property was included in a covenant prohibiting tenancy by Negroes. There is no statutory definition of a Negro in New York, and Mr. Hays was able to obtain an affidavit from Professor Franz Boas, the celebrated head of the Anthropology Department at Columbia University, that a Negro is "a human being with one hundred per cent African blood."

The words whose definitions have been fixed by statute are naturally few. Unreflecting persons are often inclined to suppose that the definition of any word is fixed by the dictionary, but this, as has already been hinted, is an illusion. There is death in the dictionary, said Lowell. Definitions are fixed by usage and context. Dictionaries follow usage; they do not decide or lead it. If there were no dictionaries (and many of the cultivated people whose preferences determine usage never consult one), meanings would be unchanged. But though dictionaries do not settle meanings, they act as anchors or stabilisers in restricting changes in meaning.

It is important in many fields of study, and not least in the law, to get a firm grasp of the fact that abstract words have no fixed or "correct" meanings. The theory, for example, that there is such a thing as *justice* that exists independently of human minds, and that the business of the law is to find out what it is, will not stand examination. The theory is a modern representative of Plato's philosophical concept of universals, and survives partly as a naive idea that if there is a name for a thing the thing must exist, and partly (as is persuasively argued in Jerome Frank's *Law and the Modern Mind*) as a relic in adults of the childish desire for certainty and fixity in a changeable and difficult world.

Much the same may be said about the abstract word *democracy*. The relationships represented by this word are those which the citizens of a country bear to each other and to their government. These relationships distinguish an autocratic country from a democratic one. It must however be admitted that one man's thoughts on these relationships will certainly not be the same as another man's. The resemblance between A's thoughts and B's thoughts is close enough to make the word *democracy* useful in discussion, though not close enough for them always to avoid controversies about what it "really means." An abstract word has no "correct meaning," never has had one, never will have one, and in the nature of things never can have one. For the lawyer, semantics has no more useful lesson.

It is a lesson that is very far from being universally understood, by lawyers or anyone else. . . . One fallacy prevalent among the learned is that the "true" meaning of a word can be discovered from the derivation, and that the word *radical*, for instance, "really means" someone who wants to get to the root of things. An amusing exploitation of the fallacy is quoted by Wellman in *The Art of Cross-Examination*. A young man who had been injured in a railroad accident was examined by the railroad doctor, who declared that the injury to his nervous system was merely hysterical, and would probably disappear in a short time. The cross-examination of the doctor by the patient's counsel, Benjamin F. Butler, is recorded as follows in Butler's autobiography:

Mr. Butler: Do I understand that you think this condition of my client wholly hysterical?

Witness: Yes, sir; undoubtedly.

And therefore won't last long?

No, sir; not likely to.

Well, doctor, let us see; is not the disease called hysteria and its effects hysterics; and isn't it true that hysteria, hysterics, hysterical, all come from the Greek word 'υστερα?

It may be.

Don't say it may, doctor; isn't it? Isn't an exact translation of the Greek word 'υστερα the English word "womb"?

You are right, sir.

Well, doctor, this morning when you examined this young man here, did you find that he had a womb? I was not aware of it before, but I will have him examined over again and see if I can find it. That is all, doctor; you may step down.

Since, however, language has to be put to practical use, and since the interpretation of the laws is the duty of the courts, lawyers and judges are frequently obliged to make estimates, which may afterwards have the force of law, as to the "true" meaning of certain words and phrases. Unfortunately, the situation to which the law has to be applied is seldom one that could have been in the minds of the legislators who framed it. In the eighteenth century, for example, lawmaking bodies could not have foreseen that their laws would have to be applied to the distribution of electric power. The court has then to decide how they would have intended the law to apply if they had been acquainted with the situation. The task of making such decisions may be one to exercise the keenest intellects in the profession. Before giving examples of the efforts of advocates to interpret words in some desired sense, we may quote passages from two masterly judicial interpretations, made by Justice Holmes, of phrases in the Constitution of the United States.

The first, delivered when Holmes was a justice of the Supreme Court, deals with the constitutional guarantee of "the equal protection of the laws." The question to be settled was, whether the state of Virginia had the right to sterilise mentally defective patients in an asylum. The court decided that it had. *Buck v. Bell*, 274 U.S. 200 (1927); Holmes, J., for the Court.

We have seen more than once that the public welfare may call upon the best citizens for their lives. It would be strange if it could not call upon those who already sap the strength of the state for these lesser sacrifices, often not felt to be such by those concerned, in order to prevent our being swamped by incompetence. It is better for all the world, if instead of waiting to execute degenerate offspring for crime, or to let them starve for their imbecility, society can prevent those who are manifestly unfit from continuing their kind. The principle that sustains compulsory vaccination is broad enough to cover cutting the Fallopian tubes. *Jacobson v. Massachusetts*, 197 U.S. 11. Three generations of imbeciles are enough.

But, it is said, however it might be if this reasoning were applied generally, it fails when it is confined to the small number who are in the institutions named and is not applied to the multitudes outside. It is the usual last resort of constitutional arguments to point out shortcomings of this sort. But the answer is that the law does all that is needed when it does all that it can, indicates a policy, applies to all within the lines, and seeks to bring within the lines all similarly situated so far and so fast as its means allow. Of course so far as the operations enable those who otherwise must be kept confined to be returned to the world, and thus open the asylum to others, the equality aimed at will be more nearly reached.

A careful reader will not fail to note the sarcasm in the final sentence of this opinion.

The second specimen of Holmes's interpretations of the Constitution dates from 1901, when he was Chief Justice of the Supreme Court of Massachusetts. In 1898 a statute had been passed in Massachusetts which replaced hanging by electrocution. The first criminal to be sentenced to death after the enactment of the statute appealed, on the ground that the Constitution of the United States forbad "cruel and unusual punishments" and that electrocution was unusual. Penal electrocution, as a novelty in Massachusetts, incontestably was unusual, but the Court held that *unusual* must be taken with *cruel* — an excellent example of the principle that meaning depends on context, *Storti v. Commonwealth*, 178 Mass. 549 (1901); Holmes, C. J., for the Court:

> The answer to the whole argument which has been presented is that there is but a single punishment, death. It is not contended that if this is true the statute is invalid, but it is not true, and that you cannot separate the means from the end in considering what the punishment is, any more when the means is a current of electricity than when it is a slow fire. We should have thought that the distinction was plain. In the latter case the means is adopted not solely for the purpose of accomplishing the end of death but for the purpose of causing other pain to the person concerned. The so-called means is also an end of the same kind as the death itself, or in other words is intended to be a part of the punishment. But when, as here, the means adopted are chosen with just the contrary intent, and are devised for the purpose of reaching the end proposed as swiftly and painlessly as possible, we are of the opinion that they are not forbidden by the Constitution although they should be discoveries of recent science and never should have been heard of before. Not only is the prohibition addressed to what in a proper sense may be called

106

the punishment but, further, the word *unusual* must be construed with the word *cruel* and cannot be taken so broadly
as to prohibit every humane improvement not previously
known in Massachusetts.

Forensic ingenuity of the same type, though applied to a
less tragic situation, appeared in the *New Yorker* of December
7, 1946, in an account of the well-known New York law firm
of Howe and Hummel. The firm was retained to defend three
Philadelphia gypsies who had been arrested for performing
a *danse de ventre*, described as a "lewd and lascivious con-
tortion of the stomach." The stomach, however, said Hummel,
was merely a small sac in the abdominal region, whose con-
tortions, if any, could not be perceived except from inside the
body. The case was dismissed.

The meaning of a word may be completely altered by differences in tone and emphasis, and these differences, if made
clear by an able lawyer, can sometimes change the whole complexion of a case. Sir Edward Marshall Hall delivered some
wonderfully acute expositions of this sort, recorded in the
biography by Edward Marjoribanks, *For the Defense*. In 1900
he appeared at the Assizes at Guildford, near London, to
defend a young unmarried woman on the charge of murder-
ing her baby. She had been seduced by a married man, and
before the birth of her child she left her home and found work
as a laundress in another part of England. The child died ten
days after birth, probably from being accidentally overlaid
by the mother. She put the body in a box and left the neigh-
borhood, but she was traced, and to the detective who questioned her she said, "I will tell you the truth. I killed it — I
did not know what do do with it — I put it in a box; you will
find it there." The body was found, and the mother was charged
with willful murder, which she confessed to the police inspec-

tor who charged her — or so said the prosecution. Under cross-examination, however, the inspector admitted that he had never charged her with the willful murder of the child, but merely with causing its death. But the prisoner had to explain still another, and a more serious, admission. Shortly before taking the child up to bed with her on the last night of its existence, she said to the nurse who was sitting with them, "How can anyone get rid of a baby?" Marshall Hall's virtuosity in presenting the true meaning of these two admissions is a beautiful example of what can be done by a lawyer sensitive to the possibilities of the spoken language.

By cross-examination of the nurse he showed that the actual words used by the prisoner were "How can anyone get rid of a little baby like this!," and that the stress fell on the word *can*. The nurse also agreed that when the words were spoken the mother was kissing and fondling and actually feeding the child, behavior which, when taken with the altered stress of the sentence, made it seem most improbable that she was asking for advice as to how to murder it. The meaning of the admission to the detective is altered by a change in punctuation: "I killed it. I did not know what do do with it; I put it in a box." In the sentence "I did not know what to do with it" goes with "I put it in a box," the admission is much less detrimental than if it goes with "I killed it."

Marshall Hall's defence convinced the judge. "There is no doubt," said the judge, "that the prisoner was fond of her child. In the whole of my experience I have never known a case where accent had greater significance. I confess that when I read the depositions taken at the inquest I thought the girl's words were meant as an enquiry, but what Mrs. Deaker said before the magistrates was exactly consistent with what she said this morning, namely, "How *can* anyone get rid of a baby like this!' with the accent on the 'can.' This puts an entirely different complexion on the matter. With regard to the prisoner's admission to the police-inspector, that is a very serious illustration of the difference punctuation may make to the meaning of words. 'I killed it — I did not know what to do with it.' If you make a pause there, and then go on, 'I put it in a box,' the phrase is an ugly one, inasmuch as it is perfectly consistent with, 'I killed it *because* I did not know what to do with it.' If, however, you pause after 'I killed it,' and proceed, 'I did not know what to do with it, and I put it in a box,' the import of the phrase is not nearly so serious." The jury found the prisoner not guilty without leaving the box.

Questions for Discussion

1. Select several abstract words, such as "freedom," "justice," and "love," and check their denotative meanings. Discuss what common usage dictates as compared with your connotations for these words.
2. Why are customs often continued after the beliefs they were based on have passed away? Specifically, what are some of the "many plausible reasons" for witnesses in court to lift their right hands as they take an oath?
3. Why do you think there are so few words whose definitions have been fixed by statute?
4. Explain the concept advanced by I. A. Richards that the meaning of a word is the missing part of its context.
5. Briefly discuss the semantic problems suggested by the cases described in this selection.

6. Gilbert Highet has said, "To simplify history is to falsify it." Can you think of instances when the omission of details distorts the facts?

Writing Assignments

1. Think of another profession in which semantic sense would be important to success. Compose a paper in which you discuss, as did Philbrick, the importance of "interpretation" to this profession.
2. Many of us have a habit of appraising objects, people, and actions, indeed everything that arouses our senses or thought processes, with the following terms: good-bad, up-down, black-white, success-failure. Make a list of your own dichotomies. What is often wrong with using these opposites as evaluations?
3. Write a brief, favorable review of a recent movie you have seen or of a book you have read; then write an unfavorable review of this same movie or book. Insofar as is possible, use the same facts for each review. Read your papers aloud. Discuss with other class members what you have learned from this assignment.
4. Sometimes we are told that the problems of the world are essentially "political" or "moral" or "economic." Attempt to define what is meant by such statements. Explain to what extent they are a comment on the person making the statement.

Selected Bibliography

Bridgman, P. W., *The Way Things Are*, Harvard University Press, Cambridge, Mass., 1959.

Chase, Stuart, *The Tyranny of Words*, Harcourt, Brace & World, New York, 1938.

Fabun, Don, *Communications: The Transfer of Meaning*, Glencoe Press, Beverly Hills, Ca., 1968.

Flesch, Rudolph, "The Rise and Fall of Formal Logic," *The Art of Clear Thinking*, Harper & Row, New York, 1951.

Gordon, Theodore, "Bucking the Scientific Establishment," *Playboy Magazine*, April 1968.

Hayakawa, S. I., *Language in Thought and Action*, Second Edition, Harcourt, Brace & World, New York, 1964.

Johnson, Wendell, *People in Quandaries*, Harper & Row, New York, 1946.

Korzybski, Alfred, *Manhood of Humanity*, Second Edition, Institute of General Semantics, Lakeville, Conn., 1950.

Korzybski, Alfred, *Science and Sanity*, Fourth Edition, Institute of General Semantics, Lakeville, Conn., 1958.

Lee, Irving, *Language Habits in Human Affairs*, Harper & Row, New York, 1941.

Mausner, Bernard and Judith, "A Study of the Antiscientific Attitude," *Scientific American*, February 1955.

Miller, Ward, *Word Wealth*, Holt, Rinehart & Winston, New York, 1967.

Ogden, C. K. and I. A. Richards, *The Meaning of Meaning*, Harcourt, Brace & World, New York, 1923.

Postman, Neil, and Charles Weingartner, "Semantics," *Linguistics: A Revolution in Teaching*, Dell, New York, 1966.

Salomon, Louis, *Semantics and Common Sense*, Holt, Rinehart & Winston, New York, 1966.

Stevenson, Ian, "Scientists With Half-closed Minds," *Harper's Magazine*, November 1958.

Thomas, Cleveland, *Language Power for Youth*, Appleton-Century-Crofts, New York, 1955.

Whitehead, Alfred North, *The Aims of Education*, Macmillan, New York, 1959.